Advance Praise for *Glad We Met*

"Steven Rogelberg knows more about how to improve meetings than anyone on earth. If you've ever lamented that a meeting could've been an email, this book is filled with data and practical advice for making the time we spend together less miserable and more worthwhile."

—**Adam Grant**, PhD, #1 New York Times bestselling author of *Think Again* and *Hidden Potential*, and host of the TED podcast WorkLife

"Starting, growing, and maintaining any business requires attracting and nurturing good people. And one of the best—and also most underutilized—tools in fostering talent is the 1:1 meeting. In this highly practical book, meetings expert Steven Rogelberg shares powerful science to inform and elevate these crucial interactions. Read *Glad We Met*—you and your team will be glad you did!"

—**Arianna Huffington**, Founder & CEO, Thrive Global

"The world's leading scholar of meetings unpacks the most important meeting of all—direct conversations between managers and team members. Rooted in deep research and replete with actionable takeaways, this book will transform how—and why—you conduct these essential encounters. *Glad We Met* is an urgent read for anyone trying to find their footing on the modern workplace's new terrain."

—**Daniel H. Pink**, #1 New York Times bestselling author of *To Sell is Human* and *Drive*

"Steven Rogelberg is one of the most important leadership thinkers writing today. This book is insightful and compelling. Rogelberg reveals how the real work in leadership is done in conversations—sense checking, creating engagement, and building trust."

—**Dean Stamoulis**, PhD, Managing Director, Russell Reynolds Associates

"I learned so much from *Glad We Met*! One-on-one meetings will never go out of style because they are the bedrock of relationships, and I'm so glad Steven Rogelberg has compiled this authoritative guide to how to do them best!"

—**Angela Duckworth**, PhD, Rosa Lee and Egbert Chang Professor at the University of Pennsylvania and author of #1 *New York Times* bestseller, *Grit: The Power of Passion and Perseverance*

"One-on-one meetings between managers and direct reports can make or break a team. Rogelberg shows, step by step, how to use these meetings to enhance work satisfaction and productivity. This is a very valuable book!"

—**Carol Dweck**, PhD, Lewis and Virginia Eaton
Professor of Psychology, Stanford University;
author of *Mindset: The New Psychology of Success*

"The book is amazing! It's everything I never knew and I always wanted to know about 1:1s! Whether you're just starting out as a manager, or are a senior executive, a recent graduate, or have decades of experience, *Glad We Met* is a must read."

—**Adam Husein**, Senior Vice President,
Global Enterprise Data Science, Analytics, and
Social Intelligence, Warner Bros. Discovery

"We extend our minds and enhance our intelligence by thinking in concert with other people—and one of the best ways to do this is to meet one on one. In *Glad We Met*, Steven Rogelberg makes a powerful case for crafting our 1:1 meetings with more care and intention. Drawing on decades of research, he provides a blueprint for making such meetings effective and productive. This book is a must-read for any manager who wants to lead a team to success."

—**Annie Murphy Paul**, author of the Washington Post bestseller
The Extended Mind: The Power of Thinking Outside the Brain

"You grow your people to grow your organization—a seedbed of that growth is the 1:1 meeting. This frequently unprepared for, often canceled, and seemingly inconsequential meeting can be, when deliberately done, a valuable investment in people and one that makes them feel genuinely seen. That's where Steven Rogelberg's evidence-based, decades-in-the-making, action-oriented approach to 1:1s comes in. Every manager (and parent) should read this book now. Your people and your organization will be glad you did."

—**Whitney Johnson**, CEO, Disruption Advisors,
Top #10 Management Thinker, Thinkers50, *WSJ*
and *USA Today* bestselling author of *Smart Growth:
How to Grow Your People to Grow Your Company*

"It is clear that many if not most leaders struggle with carrying out their 1:1 meetings. Making matters worse, leaders often have a blind spot, with their perceptions of 1:1s being more positive than what their directors have to say. To help rectify this situation and promote the incredible potential of 1:1s, Steven Rogelberg offers compelling and practical evidence-based guidance for 1-1 meetings worth everyone's time and effort. This is a must-read for leaders, workers, and teammates around the globe."

—**Alex Alonso**, PhD, Chief Knowledge Officer,
Society for Human Resource Management (SHRM)

"If world leaders read this book and led 1:1 meetings with greater collaboration and impact, the world would be more peaceful and prosperous. Until then, you should read this book to improve your own approach to management and leadership."

—**Asheesh Advani**, CEO, Junior Achievement Worldwide

"*Glad We Met* can fundamentally change and improve lives at work. It brings a rich, robust, and surprising science to bear on a critical leadership activity—the 1:1 Meeting. All leaders should read this book. All coaches should read this book."

—**Matt Mochary**, CEO Coach, CEO of Mochary Method Inc. and author of bestselling book, The Great CEO Within: The Tactical Guide to Company Building

"Based on extensive research, Steven Rogelberg discusses incredibly well why effective 1:1 meetings lead to improved personnel performance and happiness, and are critical to business success. This superb book is for anyone who manages people, and for any business that wants to succeed."

—**Elizabeth F. Churchill**, PhD, Senior Director, Google

"*Glad We Met* is a game changer for leaders of all levels. It casts a bright light on the importance of the 1:1 meeting and how these meetings impact both individuals and the overall team. It is a delight to read, grounded in science and contains highly practical tips and stories."

—**Robin Cohen**, PhD, Head of Talent Management Pharmaceuticals and Enterprise R&D, Johnson & Johnson

"After reading this book, you will think differently about 1:1 meetings! *Glad We Met* provides highly compelling tools and strategies to help you unlock the full potential of your 1:1 meetings to build stronger relationships, and ultimately create a more human-centered workplace culture. This is a must read."

—**Jennifer Fisher**, Chief Well-being Officer, Deloitte & bestselling author of *Work Better Together: How to Cultivate Strong Relationships to Maximize Well-Being and Boost Bottom Lines*

"*Glad We Met* shows how 1:1s might be the most powerful way to build trust and inspire individual performance and engagement, yet arguably is the least developed tool in a People Leader's toolkit. Dr. Rogelberg does a masterful job of conveying the art and science of 1:1 meetings and equipping managers with a simple, pragmatic and actionable playbook that they can implement immediately."

—**Josh Greenwald**, SVP, CHRO TIAA Retirement Solutions

"Rogelberg does an incredible job making the case that the 1:1 meeting should not be taken for granted by leaders. He provides highly compelling evidence-based insights designed to made 1:1s highly effective and positively impactful for all parties. No matter what leadership level you are, you will be very glad you read this book."

—**Dave Burwick**, CEO, The Boston Beer Company

"Humans have survived and thrived through the stories they tell and the connections they make with each other about their lived experience. At work and in life outside of work, small actions can produce oversized impact. As Lao Tzu prophetically noted, 'Great acts are made up of small deeds.' Professor Rogelberg poignantly and persuasively reminds us that one of the most common practices at work, one-on-one meetings, is precisely one of those 'small deeds' that contribute to 'great acts.' This evidence-based book is replete with actionable advice that can move one-on-one meetings from the mundane to the fuel that can literally transform individuals, teams, and organizations."

—**David Altman**, PhD, Chief Research & Innovation Officer, Center for Creative Leadership

"A fantastic, enjoyable book, packed with unique evidence-based insights. *Glad We Met* can absolutely elevate work life for both leaders and teams. A must read!"

—**Tasha Eurich**, PhD, New York Times bestselling author of *Insight and Bankable Leadership*

"*Glad We met* does for one-on-one meetings what *The Surprising Science of Meetings* did for standups and work sessions. At last, there is a research-backed but highly practical step-by-step guide to make the most the time you have with your direct reports. As Rogelberg keenly notes – the one-on-one meeting can be the foundation of your relationship with your team members, but only if done well. *Glad We Met* provides a roadmap on how to make these meetings useful and fulfilling for leaders and team members, alike."

—**Stephanie Johnson**, PhD, Professor and Director, Doerr Institute for New Leaders and author of the WSJ bestseller, *Inclusify: The Power of Uniqueness and Belonging to Build Innovative Teams*

"1:1s can make or break your team, your culture, and your company. In this must-read guide for managers, Dr. Rogelberg explains the evidence-based simple steps you can take to make sure every 1:1 makes you and your team better."

—**Laszlo Bock**, former CHRO of Google and founder of Humu and Gretel.ai

"Refreshingly practical, this book is the definitive guide for making meetings work– especially those all-important one-on-one meetings with people who depend on you to perform and thrive. Author Steven

Rogelberg, the leading expert in the important and understudied topic of meetings, offers actionable advice that will make anyone a better manager."

—**Amy Edmondson**, PhD, Novartis Professor of Leadership and Management, Harvard Business School and author of the bestseller, *The Fearless Organization*

"With an approachable tone and loads of pragmatic tools and templates, Steven Rogelberg's new book on that most ubiquitous meeting type, 1:1's, is essential reading. As with his prior book on meetings, this is well-researched and grounded in solid science, but still accessible and relevant. While written to managers, this book is also useful for those who actually own those meetings—the team member."

—**Alexis Fink**, PhD, Vice President, People Analytics and Workforce Strategy, Meta and President-Elect of the Society for Industrial and Organizational Psychology

"In this era of global uncertainty and conflict, massive change, technological advances, disengaged workers, burnout and a complete reimagination of the role 'work' plays in each of our lives, Steven's book is a timely reminder of the core responsibility of a manager . . . to connect an employee to the mission and purpose of the organization, understand their role in the organization' success, to support him or her to deliver superior work that drives business results and to unleash their inner greatness. While the setting, frequency or length may vary, it starts with a caring, empathetic manager who sends powerful messages about support, inclusion, performance and excellence during thoughtful, planned meetings and about becoming the best at the job at hand and preparing for the career advancements that lie ahead. This book is a must-read roadmap for managers to successfully take employees on that journey."

—**Rebecca L Ray**, PhD, Executive Vice President, Human Capital, The Conference Board

"So many of us miss the opportunity to use 1-1 meetings as the powerful tool they are. Thankfully, Steven Rogelberg has created the definitive guide to leading radically useful 1-1s that can build relationships and transform your connections with colleagues, team members, and your own manager."

—**Dorie Clark**, Wall Street Journal bestselling author of *The Long Game* and executive education faculty, Duke University Fuqua School of Business

"*Glad We Met* is an incredibly exciting and rare work that sheds a bright light on a critical work activity too often taken for granted—the 1:1 Meeting. Its evidence-based insights are highly compelling and can be leveraged to truly change the work lives of your team and by doing so promote success for you and your organization. This is a must read."

—**Robert Pasin**, CEO, Radio Flyer

"*Glad We Met* may be one of the most helpful, valuable, practical, and grounded leadership books of the year. It is insightful and a joy to read. More importantly, it is *useable.* Rogelberg leverages cutting edge science to guide leaders to make 1:1 meetings truly work to promote employee and leader thriving."

—**Peter Bregman**, CEO Bregman Partners and bestselling author of *18 Minutes* and *Leading with Emotional Courage*

"My introduction to Steven was catalyzing. He packed practical, science-based wisdom into an engaging 1-hour keynote based on his excellent book, *Glad We Met.* Through Steven, we've taught my company, and now our clients, that your success in a 1:1 is equal to your success as a leader. 1:1's are the stage upon which you solve your complex work problems as well as where you set your leadership brand, and create a psychologically safe environment to connect, coach, develop, retain talent, and combat burnout."

—**Tacy M. Byham**, PhD, Chief Executive Officer, DDI and co-author of *Your First Leadership Job*

"Are you looking for a way to truly connect with your team and help them achieve their highest potential? Look no further than Glad We Met. In this book, Dr. Rogelberg offers a unique perspective on how stewardship of time and talent through effective one-on-ones nurture professional growth and lead to meeting high and hard-to-achieve goals."

—**Aldo Zanoni,** CEO of Riva International and Co-Founder of Kairos - Software for Meetings in a Hybrid World

"This highly compelling book provides a very practical and research driven blueprint for how to go about achieving effective 1:1s. And guess what - that value is in the eyes of the recipient, not those of the manager. Managers are there to support and to help their directs be at their best. A great read for anyone wanting to know how to best engage with those they work with, and by doing so, reach new heights as a manager."

—**Matthew Saxon**, Chief People Officer, Zoom Video Communications

Glad We Met

The Art and Science of 1:1 Meetings

Steven G. Rogelberg

OXFORD
UNIVERSITY PRESS

OXFORD
UNIVERSITY PRESS

Oxford University Press is a department of the University of Oxford. It furthers the University's objective of excellence in research, scholarship, and education by publishing worldwide. Oxford is a registered trade mark of Oxford University Press in the UK and certain other countries.

Published in the United States of America by Oxford University Press
198 Madison Avenue, New York, NY 10016, United States of America.

Library of Congress Cataloging-in-Publication Data
Names: Rogelberg, Steven G., author.
Title: Glad we met : the art and science of 1:1 meetings / Steven G. Rogelberg.
Description: New York, NY : Steven Rogelberg, [2024] |
Includes bibliographical references and index.
Identifiers: LCCN 2023019465 (print) | LCCN 2023019466 (ebook) |
ISBN 9780197641873 (hardback) | ISBN 9780197641897 (epub) |
ISBN 9780197641903
Subjects: LCSH: Business meetings. | Staff meetings. |
Communication in management. | Interpersonal communication.
Classification: LCC HF5734.5.R64 2024 (print) | LCC HF5734.5 (ebook) |
DDC 658.4/56—dc23
LC record available at https://lccn.loc.gov/2023019465
LC ebook record available at https://lccn.loc.gov/2023019466

DOI: 10.1093/oso/9780197641873.001.0001

Printed by Sheridan Books, Inc., United States of America

This book is dedicated to two amazing, kind, loving, inspirational, supportive, and generous women—my Mom, Jane Rogelberg, with whom I had my very first 1:1 meeting, and my wife, Sandy Rogelberg, with whom I have had the most 1:1s by far.

Contents

Foreword

By Dr. Marshall Goldsmith

As an Executive Coach for over 40 years, my mission has been to work with leaders to create positive, lasting change for themselves, their teams, and their organizations. At the heart of effective leadership is the trust and communication that executives build with their team members. Although this trust is built through many important behaviors and actions, one of the practices all of my clients go through is a process called feedforward.

Early in my career, it became very clear that leaders and their direct reports were in desperate need of consistent and timely feedback on their progress and performance. But getting my leaders to conduct these sessions with their reports felt like pulling teeth. Many associated feedback with focusing on the past, bringing up failures, and having difficult conversations that were challenging to approach. As a result, the reports never got any meaningful follow-up, and their performances suffered. 1:1 meetings were dreaded and signaled that there would be negative topics and emotions discussed.

Feedforward takes the fear and discomfort out of feedback by focusing on ideas and suggestions for the future. Each leader is required to have consistent one-on-one meetings with their reports not only to follow up on the status of their work, but also to provide ideas on changes for the future. Key to this process is that the leader also asks for ideas for their own leadership and invites their employees to think of ways they can implement better leadership behaviors in the future. This element of not only giving, but also asking to receive advice for the future opened the door for increased humility and communication in a way I hadn't seen before.

One of the surprising outcomes to feedforward was that creating these 1:1 meetings with at least one agenda item that focused on personal and professional development gave the space the leaders and employees needed to present other questions and concerns and to collaborate on much more than they felt comfortable doing before. These became highlight moments of the week for my clients. They felt better connected with each of their direct reports and enjoyed increased engagement and growth from their entire team. This small change made 1:1 meetings the pillar of their leadership and radically changed their cultures and productivity as a whole.

Unlocking the full potential and benefits for successful 1:1 meetings, Steven's latest book allows you to create these spaces within your own teams to connect and grow meaningfully. By answering such questions about whether you really need to have 1:1 meetings, what they should cover, and how you should conduct them, *Glad We Met* ensures you walk away with the tools you need to start leading better meetings today. The benefits from these improved meetings will go far beyond better productivity for team culture, communication, and engagement.

Steven's expert knowledge in coaching and helping leaders build trust and positive communication over the last 20 years is invaluable for this book. His extensive research on this topic provides critical insights and an evidence-based approach. Filled with actionable steps and real examples to help you learn, this material is applicable across a wide range of meetings with different types of people, even beyond managers and team members.

Start investing in your team and cultivating the positive, trusting culture with *Glad We Met*!

- Dr. Marshall Goldsmith is the *Thinkers50* #1 Executive Coach and *New York Times* bestselling author of *The Earned Life*, *Triggers*, and *What Got You Here Won't Get You There*.

Preface: Vision, Approach, and the Science

There's a hole the size of the Grand Canyon when it comes to 1:1s

David Rodriguez, Board Director & Chief HR Officer, Marriott International (Retired)

As an organizational psychologist I am drawn to research work phenomena that are understudied, pervasive, performed poorly, and yet highly consequential to the thriving and success of individuals and teams. This brings me squarely to the topic of one-on-one meetings (1:1s) as it checks all these boxes for sure. My mission, collect and synthesize evidence so that the amazing potential of 1:1s can be fully realized by leaders and team members alike.

1:1s are incredibly common. Elise Keith recently did a careful analysis of overall meeting activity in the United States using archival data and a host of thoughtful extrapolations. She concluded that there are an estimated 62 to 80 million meetings per day in the United States alone.[1]

Let's expand to the rest of the world now. The United States represents just over 4% of the global population. Interestingly, in the only cross-cultural study I could find, no significant differences were found across countries in meeting activity.[2] Given this, one could make the case that to approximate how many meetings occur each day as a planet, you would need to multiply the U.S. meeting estimate by 25 times. Using Elise's low-end estimate of 62 million meetings in the United States, multiplied by 25, you get: 1.55 billion meetings a day. To be even more conservative, let's round this down and call it a billion meetings a day. My gosh, that is a lot of meetings. Next, let's hone in on 1:1s.

Based on my research and the research of others, 20% to 50% of all meetings are 1:1s[2]—that's anywhere from 200 million to 500 million 1:1 meetings each day around the world. We can attach a dollar value to these meetings. To do so, the following parameters are used: a low-end estimate of wages ($9.37 per hour based on a BBC analysis of average global wages[3]), average time for each 1:1 (20 minutes, which again is conservative based on my work), multiplied by two attendees, and the lesser estimate of 200 million 1:1s per day. Calculated together, the investment in 1:1s is 1.25 billion USD per day. Let me emphasize, this is **per day**!

Now for really troubling news, my initial research finds that nearly half of 1:1s are rated as suboptimal by team members. Nearly half. Compounding the problem, leaders' self-ratings of their skills in conducting 1:1s appear to be inflated, suggesting that leaders think they are doing a better job at leading 1:1s than they actually are. Hence, an incredible opportunity exists to fill this gap in leadership skills and to maximize the return of investment for this critical workplace activity. The problem is that despite 1:1s filling leaders' calendars, meaningful guidance on how to conduct 1:1s is quite sparse. Making matters worse, the guidance that does exist is rarely based on strong evidence and science. Instead, managers are left to rely on a) what feels right to them, b) repeating practices they have experienced by their current and former managers, and c) guesswork. The purpose of this book is to fill that gap.

Besides its evidence-based comprehensiveness, this book will help readers leverage science to navigate the difficult balancing act required in 1:1s. In the following graphic, I illustrate the foci of this balance. For example, 1:1s need structure, but also flexibility. 1:1s must tackle short-term issues, but also need to address long-term topics. 1:1s need to solve problems, but they also need to build relationships. 1:1s need to be tailored to meet the needs of the direct, but at the same time, some consistency is needed across your team. This book will provide guidance on how to balance these scales.

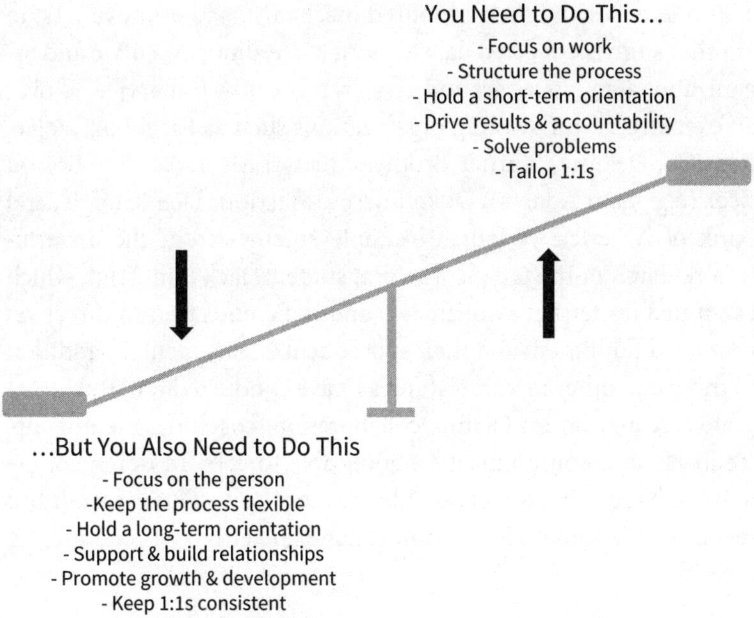
You Need to Do This…
- Focus on work
- Structure the process
- Hold a short-term orientation
- Drive results & accountability
- Solve problems
- Tailor 1:1s
…But You Also Need to Do This
- Focus on the person
-Keep the process flexible
- Hold a long-term orientation
- Support & build relationships
- Promote growth & development
- Keep 1:1s consistent

The Science on Meetings

Science . . . on meetings? Yes, there is indeed a science around understanding and improving meetings. This has been a passion area of mine for years involving dozens of collaborators around the globe, examining more meetings than I could attend in a hundred lifetimes. I have studied a variety of topics related to meetings such as meeting success, attendee fatigue, characteristics of excellent meeting leaders, lateness to meetings, how to effectively schedule meetings, key ways of designing meetings, meeting interventions to promote creativity, and much, much more. Over the last few years, my focus has turned to 1:1s. I have surveyed and interviewed thousands of team members and managers about their 1:1s. For example, a longitudinal study was conducted with tech workers tracking their 1:1s over 25 weeks along with their attitudes toward their manager. In another example, I surveyed over 4,000 knowledge workers (e.g., programmers, engineers, architects) in four countries about their

1:1 preferences and their proposed mechanisms to improve 1:1s. In another study, I collected data to learn more about executive and organizational practices around 1:1s. In this study, I interviewed over 50 executives from leading organizations such as Facebook, Volvo, PepsiCo, Deloitte, Warner Brothers, Bristol Myers Squibb, Boston Beer (e.g., Sam Adams), Duke Energy, Marriott, Dell, Google, and Bank of America. A fourth example emerges from the dissertation research of my terrific doctoral student, Jack Flinchum, which examined leader behavior in 1:1s and the connection to direct report need fulfillment and their subsequent engagement. In addition to these and other research studies I have conducted on 1:1s, I integrate research on leadership, collaboration, coaching, mentorship, feedback, and communication applicable to 1:1s. In doing so, my hope is that this book will provide the most up-to-date research and recommendations on how to understand and effectively conduct 1:1 meetings.

Book Structure

This book deeply explores the "whats," "hows," and "whys" of 1:1s by highlighting challenges, pain points, opportunities, and areas for customization. To stress the practical steps of 1:1s, each chapter is phrased as a question to be answered. The chapter then leverages science, lived experiences, and best practices of 1:1s where applicable to answer the question and to bring the content to life. The book ends with special topics such as skip-level 1:1s (a meeting with your manager's manager) and navigating the challenge of too many meetings (what meeting science researchers call "meeting load"). Finally, I provide tools throughout the book to help you succeed in your 1:1s including agenda templates, facilitation checklists, assessments to see how your skills measure up, special considerations for remote employees, and many others.

The voice I use throughout is the voice I use when giving a talk or workshop. It is conversational, a little sarcastic and silly at times, but grounded with science. The hope is that it reads like an engaging

TED Talk. Furthermore—apart from Chapter 11—I am talking to leaders of all levels throughout the book (I use the terms "leader" and "manager" interchangeably). So, when I use the term "you" in the book, it is a broad term to represent the person organizing, calling, and orchestrating the 1:1—which is typically the leader, but not always. At the same time, this book is not solely intended for those who manage other employees. Non-managers (I use the terms "team member" (TM), "direct report" (DR) or "direct" throughout the book) will absolutely benefit from the learnings as it will enable them to get more out of the 1:1s they participate in and position them well when they inevitably lead 1:1s. While I spotlight arguably the most critical type of 1:1–1:1s between leaders and their direct reports—most of the content discussed will be relevant to all types of 1:1s, from peer-to-peer to employee-to-customer. These insights can even be applied to elevating informal 1:1s between family and friends.

Before starting our journey, I want to begin by commenting on social and organizational science more broadly. Studying humans, human behavior, team behavior, and how two people (a dyad) interact is inherently complex. While patterns, insights, and learnings do emerge over time, they do not represent an absolute truth. Even with the most rigorous research, there is always more to learn, new variables to examine, new settings to explore, different people and cultures to investigate, and so much more. Therefore, science provides us with a bounded truth (i.e., what we think we know at the moment), which sets the stage for future exploration and discovery. Acting in accordance with science will tend to yield the best outcomes for you and your directs. However, given the evolving nature of science, paths not aligned with science still have the potential to work for some people, in some situations, if executed well. For example, monthly 1:1s are associated with poorer engagement outcomes compared to weekly or biweekly 1:1s. Knowing this, would I advocate monthly 1:1s based on the science? Probably not. But could this cadence work in certain circumstances depending on team size, relationship with the leader, level in the organization, and tenure together? Possibly, yes. Throughout the book

I try to emphasize evidence-based practices, but that does not mean that you can't veer in a different direction, if warranted. This book respects individual choice and tailoring. But it is better to err on the side of acting consistently with the data more times than not; it will yield better outcomes as it increases your odds of success.

Acknowledgments

One year and around 52 thousand words later, here we are. The book has been birthed. My name is on the cover, but there is a ton of wonderful people behind this all. First, thank you to my agent, Jill Marsal. Jill you have been an incredible resource and mentor to me. Next, thank you, Dana Bliss, Executive Editor at Oxford. Your never wavering support and guidance has been a true gift. Two Organizational Science Ph.D. students, now doctors, Liana Kreamer and Jack Flinchums' fingerprints are all over this book. I don't think I could have done this book without you—you both are amazing and brilliant partners. And, I love you both. Speaking of love, Sandy Rogelberg (spouse), Jane Rogelberg (mom), Sasha Rogelberg (daughter) and her partner Laney Myers, Gordon Rogelberg (son), Peter Kahn (best friend), Lynn Doran (mom in-law), and Mochi (my pug), what can I say. Thank you is not enough. You are my rocks. You are my life. I wake up each day filled with love for you all. I also want to acknowledge loved ones that shaped me greatly, but sadly have passed on. This starts with my Dad (Joel). Thank you for always challenging me, pushing me, and loving me deeply. I miss you so much and long for one more hug, one more meal, and one more laugh. And, my grandparents, your unconditional love sustained me and made me feel so safe to be the silly little boy I was (and maybe still am). My list of gratitude could go on and on and on. There are so many amazing people in my life. You know who you are as we don't hesitate to express our love and appreciation. I am a fortunate, lucky, and grateful man.

SECTION 1

SETTING THE STAGE FOR 1:1S

In this section of the book, I discuss the following: 1) why 1:1s; 2) communicating about 1:1s; 3) 1:1 cadence; 4) scheduling and location of 1:1s; 5) questions making up a 1:1; and 6) what a 1:1 agenda can look like. These topics are designed to get you on the path toward excellent 1:1s. These are the critical foundational topics to understand before you move into actually conducting the 1:1, which is Section 2 of the book.

Every 1:1 is an opportunity to make an investment in a person's development and to help them, no strings attached. The compounded effects of developmental investments, conversation by conversation, can enhance individual success and foster a healthy, productive, and resilient organizational culture.

Executive, Center for Creative Leadership

Personal and organizational effectiveness are contingent on trust that deepens with each 1:1 conducted with intentionality, focus, care, authenticity, and vulnerability. In turn, stronger and genuine connectedness fosters collective drive and success.

Admiral, U.S. Navy

1

Do I Really Need to Do 1:1s?

The answer to this question is, of course, yes. Could you imagine an author writing a book on 1:1s and then saying the answer is no? That would be a very short book, indeed. Let me alter the question to make it more difficult and nuanced.

Questions:	Yes or No
If I have regular team meetings, do I need to have 1:1s?	Y or N
If I have a good deal of social time with my team members, do I need to have 1:1s?	Y or N
If I keep my door open and emphasize my open-door policy, do I need to have 1:1s?	Y or N
If I am super responsive to emails, do I need to have 1:1s?	Y or N
If my team is doing great and my engagement scores are high, do I need to have 1:1s?	Y or N
If I have worked with my team for a long time, do I need to have 1:1s?	Y or N
If my team members aren't asking for these meetings, do I need to have 1:1s?	Y or N

The answers are still, yes, yeah, oui, sí, ja, da, and hai—that is a lot of yeses! There is something special and unique about 1:1s that goes beyond team meetings, an open-door policy, and social interactions. While this may seem exaggerated, it is not.

1:1s Are a Core Leadership Responsibility

The best leaders recognize that 1:1s are not an add-on to the job; 1:1s ARE the job of a leader. Once a leader realizes and accepts this fully, the potential of 1:1s for transforming their people and their team can start to become realized. You might already be getting heartburn at the thought of having more meetings. As someone who pretty much despises meetings (when they're poorly run), I get it. But keep in mind, well-executed 1:1s should wind up *saving* you time by creating better alignment in your team, higher performing directs, and fewer spontaneous interruptions to your workday as they are saved for the scheduled 1:1. Also, 1:1s promote employee engagement, ultimately decreasing turnover. Think about how much time and resources are spent finding and onboarding new employees. Much of that can be avoided by having effectively conducted 1:1s. With that said, 1:1s do mean having more meetings on your calendar, but these meetings are warranted and can increase efficiency in the long run.

What Is a 1:1?

In the simplest sense, 1:1s refer to **a regular and recurring time held between a manager and their directs to discuss topics such as the direct's well-being, motivation, productivity, roadblocks, priorities, clarity of roles/assignments, alignment with other work activities, goals, coordination with others/the team, employee development, and career planning.** These meetings are designed to grow and strengthen your relationship with your directs through effective, honest, and supportive communication. Ultimately, 1:1s serve to meet the practical needs of your directs, but also addresses their personal needs.[1] Practical needs refer to the support directs require to effectively conduct, prioritize, and execute their work both in the present moment and over time. Personal needs refer to directs' inherent need to be treated in a considerate way, including the need to feel respected, trusted, supported, and valued. Addressing personal and practical needs in a 1:1.is not easy. Visit the quiz assessing your overall 1:1 meetings skills found in the tools section following this book section to get a sense of your baseline.

Managers differ in how they themselves define 1:1s. For example, one manager told me that 1:1s were completely the direct's meeting. Their direct would bring him whatever topics they wanted to discuss, and they would cover those items together. Another manager told me she used 1:1 time for decision-making. She asked directs to come to every meeting with a list of decisions that they would work through. One manager used 1:1 time to provide directs with coaching. A different manager told me she does not do much coaching during her 1:1s, but focuses on more tactical problems. These are all viable approaches to 1:1s. While I would advocate for a well-rounded use of 1:1s that pretty much combines all these perspectives across time (not in a single meeting per se), there is not a "one-size-fits-all" approach to 1:1s. Success and adding real value can be achieved in a number of different ways when executed effectively and in alignment with the meeting science.

Overall, despite you driving the process to create a dedicated space on the calendar to truly engage with your people, for the most part, this is the direct's meeting. You certainly influence what is discussed and the logistics, but the meeting should be dominated by topics of importance to the team member's needs, concerns, and hopes. This is key to 1:1s—they are generally the team member's meeting, orchestrated and supported by you. One key question I often get asked is whether a formal performance appraisal meeting is a 1:1. Although this meeting type is conducted in a 1:1 format, it is really a different type of meeting.

How Do 1:1s Fit into the Performance Appraisal Process?

1:1s can elevate and complement an organization's formal performance appraisal system. In fact, 1:1s can be the engine for making a formal performance appraisal system realize its full potential for organizations. To better understand this idea, let's back up and first recognize why formal performance appraisals are needed in organizations.

A formal performance appraisal system, when done effectively, can accurately document how your people are doing. This can drive performance improvement while serving to reinforce desired behaviors through recognition of good performance. Moreover, formal assessments can be used to make better, more informed decisions about compensation, promotions, and exiting poor performers (if warranted). In the aggregate, formal performance appraisals give you a sense of your overall talent pool, where you are strong, who your high potentials are, where the bench is weak, and if you currently have the talent needed for succession planning. These appraisals can also help you determine training needs for the organization (e.g., common deficiencies that can be targeted) and serve as criteria to evaluate organizational practices such as the introduction of a new selection system or training system (e.g., did the introduction of X lead to increases in the overall performance of your people).

While there is great promise in having formal performance appraisals given these benefits, many employees—managers and directs alike—complain about them. Directs often feel the formal assessment is unfair, unbalanced, and weighted with more recent behaviors than cumulative behaviors. Directs often feel the formal assessment is not timely (e.g., the assessment may cover something that happened 6 months ago). Directs often feel anxious and stressed when wondering what will happen during the formal assessment meeting and what they will learn. Managers often dread the meetings as well and worry how their people will respond to their feedback and whether the effort truly adds value. On top of that, it is time-consuming for managers to put together a thoughtful review and complete the required documentation, especially as they may not recall all that occurred during the evaluation period for their various directs.

1:1s to the rescue. 1:1s can take anxiety out of the formal review process because performance issues and strengths have been signaled well in advance. Furthermore, notes from 1:1s serve as an incredibly helpful archive to draw from when creating a formal appraisal. Not only does this make it easier to prepare for the review, but it also increases the accuracy of your assessment and your direct's perceptions of fairness, as keeping meeting notes help to mitigate the possibility of the review being dominated by things that have happened most recently. In addition, by having 1:1s regularly, you can increase the likelihood that your people will improve over time and get the coaching they need—they can drive and enhance performance in between formal assessments. Using 1:1s in this manner should therefore make formal assessments less stressful, more valuable, and even more enjoyable for all parties.

As seen in these examples, 1:1s complement the formal performance assessment process. They become the mechanism of change, documentation, and support in real time. Also, as 1:1s help build trust and strengthen the relationships between managers and their directs, formal assessments are likely to be greeted with more open-mindedness and greater appreciation of their value.

Why 1:1s Are Critical

It cannot be stressed enough that although successful and regular 1:1s move work forward in the short term, they also promote critical outcomes that extend beyond day-to-day work. For instance, 1:1s support employee growth and development, establish trust, build the foundations of working relationships, and further still, influence how a team member fundamentally experiences you, their job, and the organization. It is not hyperbolic (well, maybe it's *a little* hyperbolic) to say that 1:1s—done well—have the potential to dramatically alter the work lives and career progression of direct reports. And although you can certainly find people who don't feel this way about 1:1s, my contention is that this view is a result of having poor experiences with 1:1s. In fact, the research is quite clear that 1:1s are arguably one of the most important activities you can do as a leader. More specifically, regularly scheduled and successful 1:1s are essential to the seven interconnected and important outcomes shown in the following figure:

Employee engagement. The link between 1:1s and employee engagement has been found in a host of contexts and studies. Gallup, for example, studied the engagement levels of 2.5 million manager-led teams around the world.[2] They found that "on average, only 15% of employees who work for a manager who does not meet with them regularly are engaged; managers who regularly meet with their employees almost tripled that level of engagement." Relatedly, in a study published in Harvard Business Review, "employees who got little to no one-on-one time with their manager were more likely to be disengaged [while] those who got twice the number of one-on-ones with their manager relative to their peers were 67% less likely to be disengaged."[3] Interestingly, research has NOT found a plateau effect for 1:1s, where too many 1:1s resulted in employee engagement leveling off or decreasing. In fact, it turns out to be just the opposite. My research generally suggests that, overall, there is a positive linear relationship, such that as the number of 1:1s increases, so does employee engagement and positive perceptions of a direct's manager.

Team member success. 1:1s are essential for promoting team member productivity and success. First, they establish a regular cadence of communication to check in on progress, create alignment, and ensure that the team member is working on the most critical projects. These meetings allow managers and team members to discuss the direct's obstacles and roadblocks, engage in real-time decision-making, enhance coordination, and provide support and resources when needed. Success is also promoted by ongoing feedback, accountability, support, and coaching. All of the above promotes the success of team members. In fact, research finds that a manager's coaching skills are positively related to directs' performance as assessed through annual sales goal attainment.[4]

Manager success. 1:1s enhance your success in three ways. First, investing time and energy in regular 1:1s decreases the need for you to answer ad hoc questions, since team members can save those questions for the 1:1 itself. This limits interruptions, increasing your ability to find longer blocks of time to focus on your work. Second, 1:1s serve as a key mechanism for you to acquire needed information, gather feedback, and communicate with your team members that better enables you to thrive and drive the team. Adam Grant summarizes the final way 1:1s promote manager success: "The higher you climb, the more your success depends on making other people successful. Leaders are judged by what their followers achieve."[5] 1:1s are clearly about helping others become more successful. This, in turn, extends to team success—which is a reflection of your success as a leader. For example, one study surveyed 1,183 managers and 838 non-managers about 1:1s. The data are striking, with 89% of managers saying that 1:1s positively affected their team's performance, and 73% of employees indicated that 1:1s positively affected their team's performance."[6]

Building relationships. Getting to know your people and engaging with them on a regular basis is the foundation of building relationships with your team. 1:1s open the door to this by providing a space to foster connection, to learn about each other, and to promote trust. They make relationship building an intentional activity—an activity that signals to your directs that they are so important to you that you are willing to schedule a meeting focused on them and their needs. At the same time, if there are problems or tension, regular 1:1s allow you and your directs to clear the air and keep your relationship on track.

Diversity and inclusion. Each 1:1 is an opportunity for you to promote—and to truly hear—the voice of your team members. A successfully conducted 1:1 provides your directs with the opportunity to be seen, connected with, and supported. 1:1s ensure each team member is not just grouped together with all other directs in the manager's mind or in their actions. Instead, 1:1s allow their unique lived experiences at work to be better understood and taken into consideration when making decisions and solving problems. As the challenges or issues of each team member are addressed in a genuine and collaborative manner, directs' ability to thrive and succeed increases—and with this success, the success of your diversity and inclusion efforts are more likely to be achieved. Given these ideas, 1:1s are an opportunity for you to fulfill your front-line role as a leader in creating an inclusive organization.

Promoting employee growth and development. Every 1:1 is an opportunity to help team members grow and develop through honest and actionable feedback, coaching, mentoring, and career conversations. Elevating those that work for you is central to being an effective leader. A quote by Jack Welch nicely summarizes this idea: "Before you are a manager, success is all about growing yourself. When you become a manager, success is all about growing others." Every 1:1 is an investment in the present and the future of your team members. At the same time, these investments across managers serve to elevate your talent pool, giving the organization a stronger bench and a greater ability to promote from within.

Life satisfaction. Research on life satisfaction consistently demonstrates the importance of helping others.[7] Doing so contributes to your overall well-being and self-concept, and even leads to better health outcomes.[8] A Chinese proverb captures this well: "If you want happiness for an hour, take a nap. If you want happiness for a day, go fishing. If you want happiness for a year, inherit a fortune. If you want happiness for a lifetime, help somebody." It's also clear from the work of Adam Grant that the most effective leaders *give* rather than *take*. 1:1s are the perfect opportunity to help others, give to others, and through both, experience the great intrinsic rewards of making a difference in the lives of others. When you have effective 1:1s, all lives are elevated—including your own.

The general assumption is that 1:1s are not for those who, say, work with their hands and use their physical abilities to complete their work (e.g., blue-collar, pink-collar, and working-class type jobs) such as construction workers, mechanics, custodial workers, truck drivers, nurses, and machine operators. I don't fully understand why anyone would feel this way. The desire to thrive, overcome obstacles, develop meaningful relationships, and feel seen/heard is not unique to any particular job type or profession. It is part of the human condition. With that in mind, my advice is to try 1:1s regardless of the job type and assess the value they provide both in the short and long term. It could very well be the case that 1:1s are good for all, but that the cadence and content of the meetings varies depending on the nature of the job type and role in question.

Let me conclude this chapter by turning this all on its head. Think about what foregoing 1:1s would convey to your people. As humans, we observe others' actions (or lack thereof) and ascribe meaning to them. Unfortunately, as we seek to make sense of what we see or don't see, research demonstrates that we are subject to a distortion bias known as the fundamental attribution error. Here is an example of this bias at play: A colleague passes you in the hallway but avoids eye contact or saying hello. Research shows that, most of the time, people would explain this behavior in dispositional terms and assume their colleague is rude, self-centered, or just aloof. These dispositional attributions tend to prevail over more nuanced situational explanations such as assuming that your colleague was distracted by an unexpected deadline or bad news. Put into the context of 1:1s, what attribution will your people make if you are not having

1:1s and other managers are? Or what if you are only having 1:1s with a select few of your directs because their job differs and you decided they need 1:1s more than your other employees? Most likely, even if you had the best of intentions in making these decisions, you will be inadvertently fostering the impression that you don't really care about your directs and their success—they are not worth the investment of your time.

Key Takeaways

- **Yes, You Need to Have 1:1s with Your Directs.** 1:1s are a regular and recurring time for you, as a manager, to meet with your directs to discuss a variety of topics. 1:1s go beyond regular team meetings, having an open-door policy, or informal interactions. Instead, 1:1s are an intentional, dedicated time for you to support your directs.
- **1:1s Are Leadership in Action.** 1:1s are not an add-on to a manager's job, they ARE a manager's job. These meetings help ensure that your directs are in the best position to succeed and that you create a healthy working relationship with each member of your team.
- **1:1s Are Not Performance Appraisals.** Performance appraisals are important, but they are not synonymous with 1:1s. Instead, 1:1s should be used to inform the performance appraisal process. Ongoing conversations and keeping notes can help align both you and your directs. In doing so, 1:1s can make performance appraisals more fair, less stressful, more effective, and even somewhat enjoyable.
- **1:1s Relate to Various Positive Outcomes.** 1:1s can promote a variety of positive outcomes for your directs, you as their manager, your team, and your organization. Some of these outcomes include improved engagement levels, team member and manager success, diversity and inclusion, relationship development, direct report growth and development, and life satisfaction.

2
Won't Team Members Be Fearful of 1:1s?

The oldest and strongest emotion of mankind is fear,
and the oldest and strongest kind of fear is fear of the unknown.

H. P. Lovecraft

People fail to get along because they fear each other;
they fear each other because they don't know each other;
they don't know each other because they have not communicated with each other.

Martin Luther King Jr.

Excellent communication and framing are essential when rolling out a new 1:1 initiative or rebooting your current approach. Without adequate communication, team members may make assumptions that can lead to misinformation and unjustified anxiety and angst. Namely, when information isn't readily apparent, we assemble clues to paint a picture of reality, and most notably, we seek out information from others to reduce this ambiguity. It is the latter that ultimately gives life to rumors that are passed through the grapevine. Interestingly, it is estimated that 70% of all organizational communication occurs at the grapevine level.[1] The grapevine often carries kernels of truth, but it tends to omit the whole truth. The grapevine can become distorted with each telling of the story, as crucial details often get left out or changed so much that the story we are left with no longer resembles the truth. This has been studied empirically in what is called *transmission chain experiments*, which is really just a fancy name for the childhood game "telephone." In this game, we sat in a circle, whispered a message to our neighbor, our neighbor whispers what they hear to the next person and so on, and by the time it gets back to the original person we see how the message has become completely distorted. Speaking to the universality of the concept, this childhood game—while named differently (see the table that follows)—is played around the world![2]

Country	Name	Translation
Turkey	kulaktan kulağa	from (one) ear to (another)
France	téléphone sans fil	wireless telephone
Germany	Stille Post	quiet mail
Malaysia	as telefon rosak	broken telephone
Israel	telefon shavur (טלפון שבור)	broken telephone
Finland	in rikkinäinen puhelin	broken telephone
Greece	halasmeno tilefono (χαλασμένο τηλέφωνο)	broken telephone
Poland	głuchy telefon	deaf telephone

Because of the potential for messaging to get distorted when transmitted informally from person to person, communicating directly with your team members is key prior to scheduling 1:1s to ensure the "whys" and "hows" are clear and potential fear is allayed. Be affirmative and principled. First, announce the roll-out (or reboot) of 1:1s to your team at a team meeting so all of your directs hear the same messaging at the same time. This will prevent anyone from feeling singled-out and ensure messaging is consistent across the team. Second, tie 1:1s to broader organizational values (e.g., importance of employee voice) and to your personal values (e.g., being a supportive leader) to contextualize the effort and signal this will be a lasting and long-term initiative. Third, stress that 1:1s aren't about micromanaging or controlling directs. Instead, make it clear that 1:1s will provide opportunities to get to know each other better, learn about challenges, discuss career development, offer help where needed, serve as a safe space to have two-way communication and exchanges, and address directs' concerns and questions. As part of the communication process, lay out what 1:1s will look like logistically. This includes cadence, time allocated, agenda creation, and location. Finally, stress that the direct will help shape these logistics over time and that you will seek their feedback to make 1:1s the best they can be.

Can having 1:1s lead a direct to feel micromanaged? It certainly can, but that is a function of your approach to 1:1s. Team members will feel micromanaged if you are indeed micromanaging them, but that is not how 1:1s are supposed to be run.

Responses to Common Questions from Team Members

To aid in your 1:1 roll out or reboot communication, here are common questions from directs and potential responses designed to inform them and allay their anxiety.

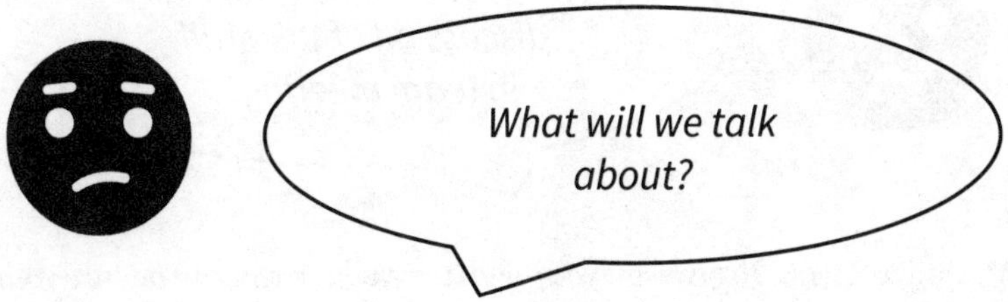

Manager: *You will shape the agenda so the 1:1 is most valuable to you. Common topics can involve a discussion of roadblocks, priorities, clarity, alignment, goals, coordination, your growth and development, and career planning. At the same time, these meetings are designed to grow our relationship.*

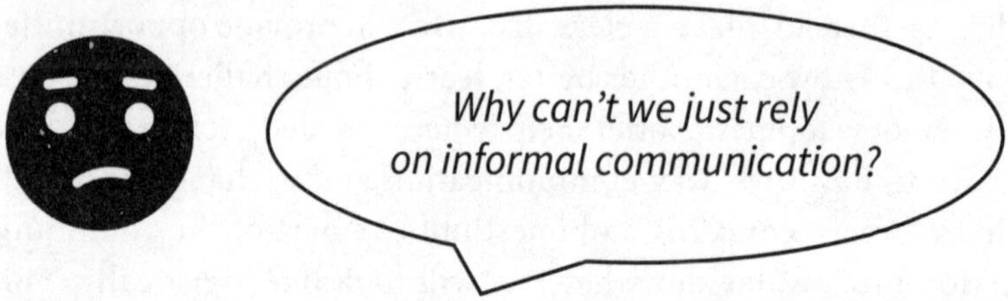

Why can't we just rely
on informal communication?

Manager: *Because we me may miss things. Furthermore, focusing on informal communication often results in a short-term focus as we will tend to prioritize fires that emerge and need to be put out instead of longer-term topics such as career growth and future planning.*

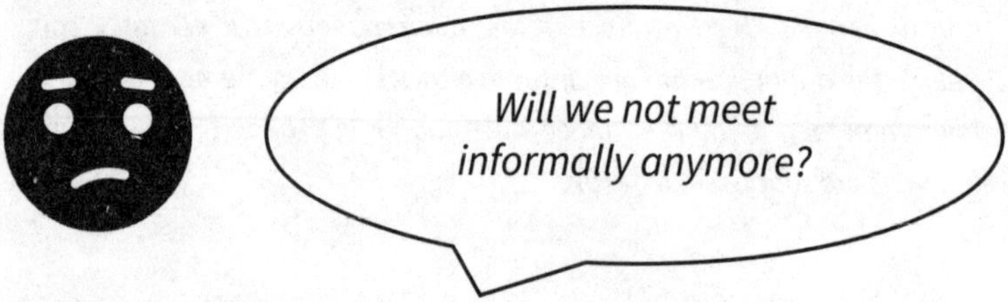

Will we not meet
informally anymore?

Manager: *1:1s don't replace our informal conversations. However, it is likely the case that we will have fewer "pop-up" meetings, since we can save certain conversations for our next 1:1. But I will continue to make myself readily available to you.*

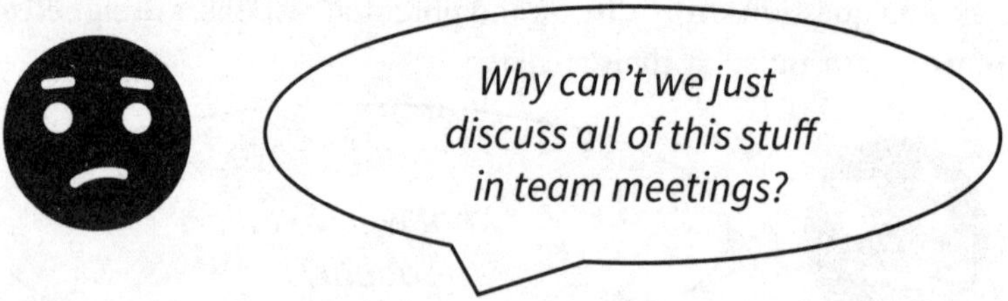

Why can't we just
discuss all of this stuff
in team meetings?

Manager: *I want to give you your own time where you can be sure your needs are met. There are additional topics, such as your career development or worries you have that can be better covered if it is just you and me. We will certainly keep the team in the loop on anything relevant to them.*

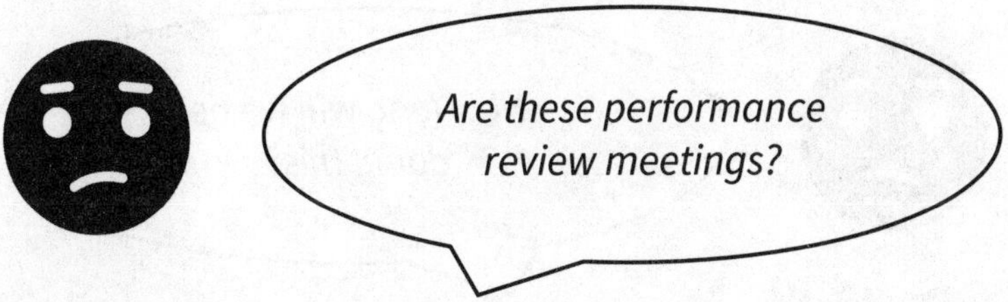
Are these performance review meetings?

Manager: *Not at all. 1:1s are definitely a great place to share feedback, do coaching, and discuss growth and development—but they are not solely focused on performance. The added benefit is that by meeting 1:1 more regularly, there are less surprises during our actual formal performance review meetings.*

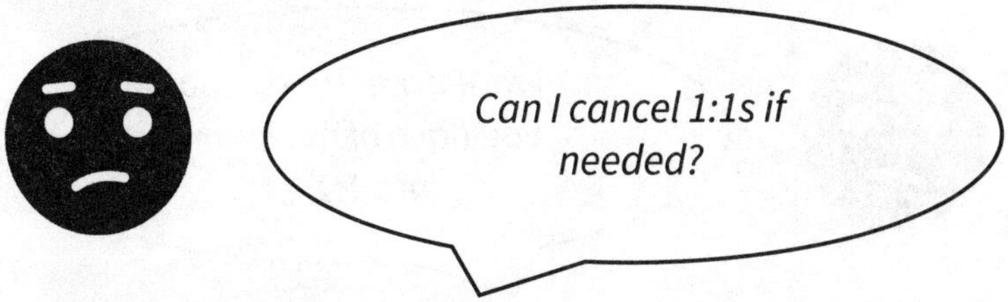
Can I cancel 1:1s if needed?

Manager: *If absolutely necessary, yes. But, it's best for us to get into a routine and stick with it. Over time, we can re-evaluate and determine the best meeting cadence for us.*

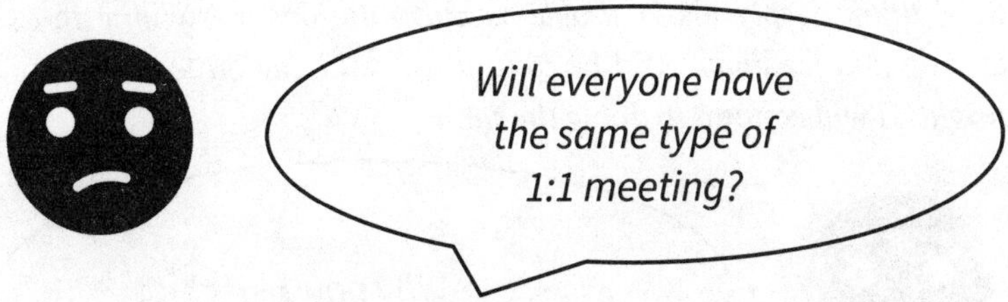
Will everyone have the same type of 1:1 meeting?

Manager: *Pretty much, yes. But given that each team member has a voice in the agenda and 1:1 process, your experience may be different from others. But the core of what a 1:1 is and how I approach them will certainly be similar.*

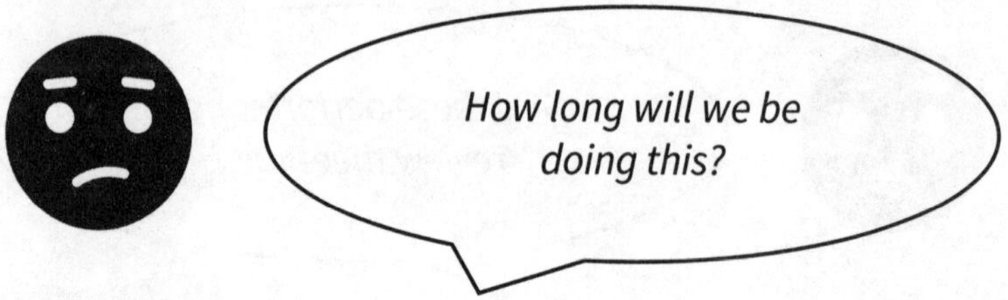

Manager: *This is not a one off. 1:1s are a fundamental part of my leadership philosophy and a way of helping build a great team. However, they can surely evolve over time to best meet your needs. To do so, we will consistently evaluate how they are working so we can tweak them and keep adding value.*

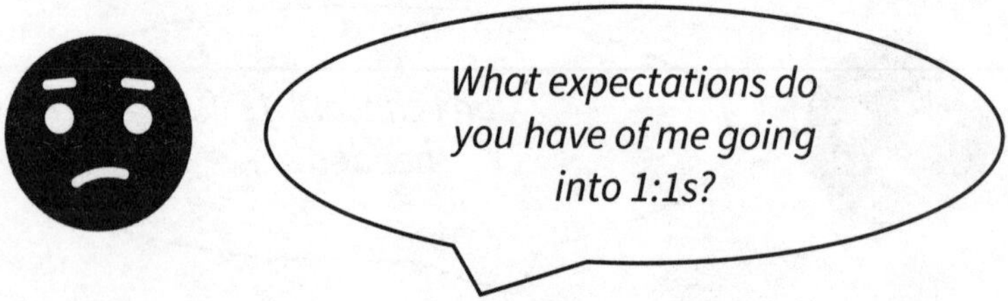

Manager: *Come open-minded and prepared. Be forthcoming with any concerns or worries so we can work through them. Drive the agenda with key priorities. Be curious, be actively engaged, communicate candidly, think deeply about problems and solutions, be willing to ask for help and feedback, and be committed to acting on learnings and insights. I will commit to doing the same.*

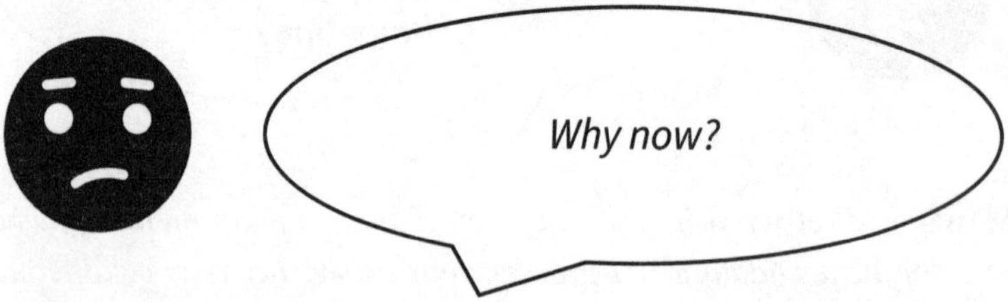

Manager: *Why wait? This is about me trying to be the best leader I can be for you, helping you grow to your greatest potential, and elevating our team.*

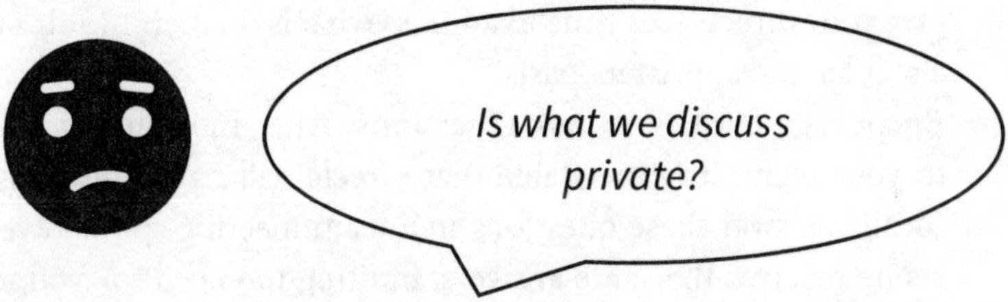
Is what we discuss
private?

Manager: *I will keep our conversation private unless told otherwise. You can do what you want in deciding what to share or not share with others. But yes, these meetings are meant to be confidential.*

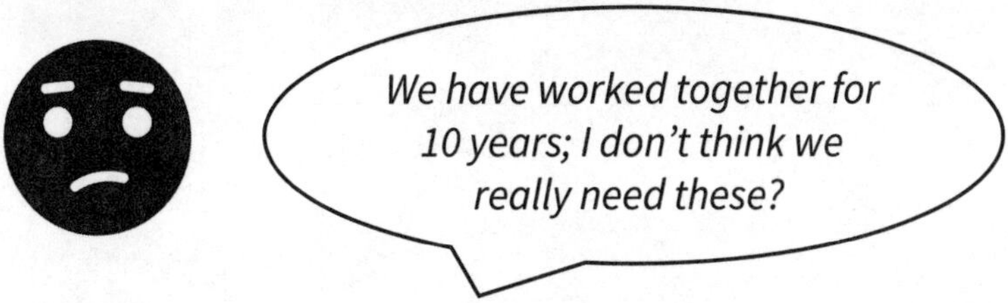
We have worked together for
10 years; I don't think we
really need these?

Manager: *You may be right. But, we don't want to take our relationship for granted. A good relationship always needs nurturing. Plus, emergent issues and problems arise that a 1:1 can allow us to address very effectively. Let's give it a good try and then commit to evaluating what is working and what is not over time to assure this is a good use of time for you.*

Key Takeaways

- **Communication Is Key for Starting 1:1s with Your Team.** When rolling out (or rebooting) 1:1s with your team, excellent communication is a necessity. To do so effectively, set up a meeting with your entire team. Give them a rundown of what 1:1s are and why you will be having them. Make it clear that all directs will be having 1:1s, tie the meetings to broader organizational and personal values, and stress that these meetings are not about micromanaging or control. Emphasize your desire to give your directs face time to address what is on their minds on a regular and consistent basis.

- **Encourage Directs to Ask Questions.** After introducing 1:1s to your team, it is inevitable that directs will have questions. Ideally, answer these questions in a team meeting so that everyone receives the same answers, limiting the need for you to repeat yourself. Common questions will concern what the meetings will be like, if having the meetings are optional, and expectations for the meetings.

3

Can't I Just Meet When I Have Something I Need to Say?

Before disclosing the science around how often to have 1:1s, let's test your knowledge with some true/false questions.

Statements:	True/False
1:1s shouldn't be held weekly as it leads to team members feeling micromanaged and over-controlled.	T/F
Employees in the feedback-hungry United States, in comparison to, say, the United Kingdom, Germany, and France, crave more 1:1s with their managers.	T/F
Given the importance of face time with your boss, those in lower levels of management express the greatest desire for 1:1s.	T/F
Without a defined 1:1 cadence plan, we tend to meet more with team members that we believe are most dissimilar to us because of an implicit bias that those different from us need the most help.	T/F
The top reason directs indicate that they want less 1:1s is meeting fatigue.	T/F

What does the evidence say? The answer to each of these questions—as you will learn throughout this chapter—is FALSE. How did you do? Surprised? So, what exactly does the science say about 1:1 meeting frequency?

Have a Plan

It starts with having a plan. You should have a strategy in place for how often you will have 1:1s with your team members, be it once a week, once every two weeks, or at another cadence. Of course, unexpected things can happen to disrupt your approach but having a 1:1 plan for your team is critical for two reasons. First, it increases the chances of a behavior occurring and, ultimately, becoming a standard routine—something that we don't think or fret much about, not unlike brushing our teeth. We just do it. The second reason centers around bias. Namely, having a plan applied across team members helps prevent two problematic biases from manifesting.

Bias one: We tend to meet more often with people who are similar to us, called the similarity-attraction bias. Research shows that we tend to feel more attracted to and trust others who we perceive as more similar to us—those with whom we share similar attitudes, physical characteristics, and personality traits—relative to those with whom we don't share these characteristics. This bias is summed up with the adage, "birds of a feather flock together." For example, research has found that shorter people tend to marry shorter partners, attractive people are more likely to marry attractive partners, and so on. If we don't have a clear 1:1 plan and instead rely on being more spontaneous and organic, this unintentional bias will likely affect our 1:1 cadence with team members. This can result in certain genders, races or ethnicities, and personality types (among other differences) not getting equal access to and treatment by you as their manager, which—even if you don't intend it to be—can be discriminatory. A 1:1 plan will help ensure you meet with all your team members relatively equally, regardless of their similarity to you.

Bias two. Seeing and interacting more with a person tends to result in us liking them more, and thus, we engage more with this person. This is called the propinquity effect, also called the mere exposure effect. Without a 1:1 plan, this could result in us privileging those we see more regularly. For example, those who work remotely may not get equal access to and treatment by us when it comes to 1:1s. This is similar to the expression, "out of sight, out of mind."

A clear 1:1 plan will help allay these idiosyncratic biases from readily taking hold.

With this all said, you can still be flexible. Namely, you can have different cadences for different people, but you want to be sure that on average (roughly), your directs get the same amount of time with you over the course of one month. For example, some team members may be at a once-a-week 1:1 cadence for 30 minutes while others may be at a biweekly 1:1 cadence for 60 minutes. This equates to the same time investment. Next, let's turn to what the research says about types of plans.

Plan Options

In my interviews with 50 executives, three plans around 1:1s were most recommended:

1. **Weekly Plan**. Once a week 1:1, for 30 minutes or so, with each team member.
2. **Biweekly Plan**. Once every other week 1:1, for 45–60 minutes, with each team member.
3. **Monthly Plan**. Every 3 or 4 weeks 1:1 for 60–90 minutes.

As for what is **normative**, some data exist. For example, the company Soapbox conducted a meetings study involving 200 managers, across a host of industries.[1] A key piece of this report examined how often 1:1s happen between a manager and a direct. The results are interesting and did not change based on organizational size or size of the leaders span of control:

Cadence	Percentage of Employees Reporting this Cadence
Weekly:	49%
Biweekly:	22%
Monthly:	15%
Quarterly:	2%

Focusing on **desired** cadences, I conducted a cross-cultural study with nearly 4,000 employees about their 1:1s. Individuals were asked: "How many 1:1 meetings would you WANT with your manager in a typical month?" Although some intriguing cross-cultural patterns emerged as you see in the following table, the overall response was four meetings per month (or weekly 1:1s). The detailed results are as follows:

Country	1:1s per month with manager (wanted)
France:	4.5
Germany:	4.6
UK:	3.3
US:	3.4
Overall	4.0

Using the same data, we also found that the higher up they were in the organization the more 1:1s per month respondents wanted with their manager.

Job level of direct	1:1s per month with manager (wanted)
Entry-level employees:	3.1
First-line supervisors:	3.7
Middle managers:	4.1
Senior managers:	4.5

Note, there was variation within each group of respondents, with some individuals wanting fewer 1:1s and some wanting more 1:1s per month. But, overall, the message is clear: **weekly 1:1s aligns most with employee preferences in general across job level and country.**

Some leaders conducted more than one 1:1 a week with their directs. The big fear with this approach is that it inadvertently results in the manager getting too "into the weeds" and micromanaging their directs, even if you don't intend for that to happen. Plus, it's just a lot of meetings. The suggestion that emerged in my interviews is that if more frequent check-ins are indeed important to the work, do more asynchronous communication (e.g., texting, Slack messaging, phone, and email) as that is typically more efficient.

To help you navigate which plan is best for you, your team, and your situation, a decision tree of sorts is presented in the list that follows. I do want to state at the onset: the data suggest that **if possible** and **reasonable**, Plan 1 (the weekly plan) in comparison to other cadences, had the most favorable outcomes. For example, in the 25-week study we conducted in the tech sector, employees with weekly 1:1s consistently rated their manager more favorably in comparison to employees with biweekly 1:1s, with scores nearly 10% higher on average. Additionally, using objective calendar data linked to an engagement survey, the weekly 1:1 cadence had the highest engagement gains, followed by the biweekly cadence, followed by less frequent cadences. Although I like weekly 1:1s given the data, I highlighted "if possible" and "reasonable" above. The question becomes: When is it not possible or reasonable to have weekly 1:1s? This brings me to a set of considerations for you to deliberate on as you create your own personal 1:1 plan for your team. The list below will help you determine the right meeting cadence for you. I also encourage you to refer to the Determine Your 1:1 Meeting Cadences quiz found in the Section 1 Tools.

- **Remote vs. In-Person.** If you have a team that is remote, a weekly cadence is recommended. This serves to counter the lack of more spontaneous contact that occurs with fully on-site teams. However, if direct reports are all or partially on-site, a case for a less frequent model can be made given the ease of informal interactions in an in-person setting.

- **Team Member Preference.** I like the idea of giving directs some voice in their 1:1 cadence. Although you can encourage weekly 1:1s, if a direct feels strongly about the biweekly option, I recommend honoring that.
- **Team Member Experience/Tenure.** If your directs are more junior and/or inexperienced, weekly 1:1s are most ideal. More frequent 1:1s allow you to provide coaching and other behaviors to support their growth and development. However, a less frequent cadence can be appropriate for directs that are more seasoned (i.e., they've worked in the company or for you for a relatively long time). Relatedly, if a team member is new to your team (even if experienced elsewhere), it is important to meet with them 1:1 on a weekly basis, at least initially. This allows you to build trust with them and will help with the onboarding process. You are a lifeline for new hires, especially in a remote environment.
- **Manager Tenure.** If you, as the manager, are new to the team, weekly 1:1s are ideal to establish relationships and alignment. If you have experience with the team, the biweekly or monthly cadence are appropriate options to consider.
- **Team Size.** If your team is quite large (perhaps 10 or more team members reporting to you), an argument for biweekly or monthly 1:1s can be made, which would allow you to stagger 1:1s across a greater window of time. In addition, you may have to dial back how much time is allotted to each meeting to help you manage your workload. For example, meet every other week for 30–40 minutes rather than for 60 minutes with each team member. Relatedly, if you have a large span of control you may need to consider structural changes to ensure your people are getting the support they need (e.g., peer mentoring and access to coaches outside the department—be it internal or paid external coaches).
- **Use of Other Technologies.** If you, as a manager, use asynchronous technologies to stay connected to your people, a

less frequent cadence could be appropriate. For example, one Google executive uses shared docs with her reports to update progress and make comments on a very frequent basis. This asynchronous communication can help decrease the need for weekly 1:1s.

- **Weekly Staff Meetings.** In the circumstance of regular, well-conducted staff meetings with a small, tight-knit team (3 or 4 directs), 1:1 meeting frequency could likely be decreased.

There is one additional factor I want to broach as it relates to 1:1 frequency: trust. Trust is not concrete like the other factors in the decision tree, but it is still key. With earned trust, it's possible that the cadence doesn't need to be as frequent, assuming the manager makes themselves available through other outlets of communication. However, I am not adding this to the decision tree, as research shows that our assessment of earned trust with others may not be fully aligned with directs. We are not necessarily the best judges of whether others trust us. What's more, earned trust is not a constant. You may have it, but you can easily lose it. It must be continuously nurtured, and you can't take it for granted.

I do want to circle back to the monthly meeting model. In many of my interviews with senior executives, they tended to rely more on the monthly 1:1 plan. Reasons given were a) large spans of control, thus too many directs to have 1:1s more frequently; b) directs were highly seasoned folks that don't need as much guidance/planning; and c) in general, their directs had been with them a long time. While the data suggests the monthly meeting cadence is not optimal relative to other cadences, it can still be helpful to directs and does yield some employee engagement gains in comparison to not having 1:1s at all. Putting aside the fact that it does not appear aligned with the preference data shared earlier where employees tend to desire more frequent 1:1s even at the senior level, there are three main reasons why this monthly model typically is not ideal: First, the time lag usually makes feedback and conversations less timely (e.g., something worthy of discussing may have occurred three weeks prior to the

1:1). Second, with monthly meetings, there is a tremendous recency bias. This bias leads to discussions of what recently happened, rather than earlier happenings during the monthly period, because recent events are easier to recall. Finally, 1:1s are most effective when they build off each other in a timely manner, as you can create momentum and alignment around developmental areas or desired actions. It is just inevitable that continuity and momentum suffer with long time lags between 1:1s. With this all said, could this monthly cadence still work given the justifications shared by executives at the top of this paragraph? Yes, but this cadence still may not be optimal. Some may ask, could a quarterly 1:1 meeting cadence be appropriate? The answer from the data appears to be generally no—in fact you could argue that a quarterly 1:1 meeting cadence doesn't really qualify as a cadence—it is really a "not meeting" plan.

The more often you have 1:1s with a direct, the shorter the meetings can be. This is why 20–30 minutes works fine for a weekly cadence. On the other hand, the less often you meet, the longer meetings will need to be (45–90 minutes) to cover everything.

Ultimately, there is no "one-size-fits-all" approach to 1:1s. Use the preceding rules of thumb to create the plan that works for you, your individual direct reports, and your unique situation. After you implement a cadence for directs, it is absolutely fine to evaluate and recalibrate over time. But try to stick to a plan for at least a couple of months to get a feel for it. After that, you will have a better sense of whether you are meeting too often, not enough, or just right.

Key Takeaways

- **Establish a 1:1 Plan for Your Team.** This ensures that you are actually having 1:1s with all team members and will help mitigate biases that could result in unconsciously favoring certain directs.

- **Find the Right Cadence.** The most common 1:1 cadences are weekly, biweekly, and monthly. Avoid having an ad hoc (as-needed) approach to the cadence of your 1:1s. Research supports weekly 1:1s as the best option in most cases.
- **Assess What's Reasonable.** To help navigate which plan is the best fit for you and your team, consider what is possible and reasonable. Things to consider include: whether you have remote team members; the preferences, experiences, and tenure of your directs; your tenure with the team; and the size of your team. There is no "one-size-fits-all" solution—choose a plan that best fits your needs and situation and adjust over time as needed.
- **Get Feedback and Adapt.** Recognize that when a direct indicates a lack of interest in 1:1s or seems interested in reducing their number, this could be a sign that 1:1s are not being conducted effectively. Continually ask for feedback on your 1:1s and consider tactics that can increase their effectiveness.

4

How Should I Schedule 1:1s—Same Day, Clustered, or Spread Out?

To answer this question, I want to first float into the concept of flow—a mental state where you are fully immersed in a task, feel absorbed by the work, and have incredible focus. In sports, this is often called being in "the zone." Mihaly Csikszentmihalyi (pronounced "chick-sent-me-hi-ee"), a psychologist, introduced flow nearly 50 years ago. He described the concept as an experience "in which people are so involved in an activity that nothing else seems to matter at the time; the experience is so enjoyable that people will do it even at great cost, for the sheer sake of doing it."[1] Research initially focused on creative professions and found that a flow state was associated with high-quality work.[2] More recently, research on flow states has been examined in a myriad of professions from managers to knowledge workers. Regardless of profession, the findings held: flow states were associated with feelings of productivity, satisfaction, and happiness at work.[3] Conversely, a lack of flow state experiences was related to negative outcomes.[4] For example, one study found that individuals who couldn't achieve flow reported feeling a sense of disorganization, having less control of their work environment, and a general sense of helplessness. Relatedly, research has shown that interrupting one's flow state causes stress, hurts productivity, and leads to increased frustration.[5] Clearly, flow is something to strive for at work.

But why are we talking about flow? Because meetings can be scheduled in a manner that works to maximize the chances of flow (and decrease interruptions). That is, if you can cluster your meetings together, like having them all in the morning, you increase opportunities for flow in the afternoon by decreasing interruptions and task-switching caused by having meetings spread throughout the day. With scattered meetings, there likely isn't enough time between meetings to accomplish your key tasks, get into a flow, or maximize your productivity. In support of this idea, research conducted with my wonderful doctoral student, Liana Kreamer, found that participants reported higher levels of anticipated productivity, accomplishment, and positive feelings when meetings were clustered together instead of spread throughout the workday. Furthermore, a study on software developers found that most respondents believed that it is more ideal to finish all daily meetings before starting any work-related tasks. In this way, the afternoon becomes an opportunity for flow. The next most-desired option was to cluster meetings in the early afternoon, given that lunch serves as a natural disruption to the workday. The morning would then be a good opportunity to achieve flow.

There are two issues to consider when using a clustering approach to your meetings.

First, make sure to build in short microbreaks between your clustered meetings to create some recovery, stretch, take a bio break, and prepare for the next meeting. One way to do this is by shortening your meetings. For example, a 30-minute meeting could be shortened to a 25-minute meeting. Second, if you worked hard to build a cluster of free time to increase your chances of flow, block it off on your calendar and try to keep it sacred. Securing this time for flow is imperative.

Although clustering meetings together appears to be most supported from a flow perspective, we still found respondents who preferred spreading out their meetings, even at the expense of flow. Some of the reasons shared were:

1. Prevent meeting fatigue caused by back-to-back meetings.
2. Allow time to decompress after meetings and reflect on meeting content/take notes.
3. Allow time to prepare for the next meeting.
4. Allow time to complete tasks or check emails in between meetings to prevent a buildup of work.

Clearly, different people will have different preferences when it comes to scheduling meetings. The reasons above are certainly understandable, but I do think they can be mitigated by adding short breaks between clustered meetings (as you see in the following figure). Still, while I would advocate for clustering meetings based on the science, if it doesn't feel right for someone, that's fine. At the very least and regardless of your preferences, consider scheduling meetings at natural break times (e.g., lunch) to minimize task-switching. Switching between tasks and refocusing is not an immediate process cognitively—it takes time and mental energy. Meetings held first thing in the morning, right before a midday break, and at the end of the day align with times when work is already naturally disrupted. This creates just one, rather than two, task-switching interruptions for each meeting. Less task-switching allows you to be more productive and feel more satisfied with your use of time, and it increases the chances of experiencing flow. Here are three examples of what the above approaches could look like on your calendar:

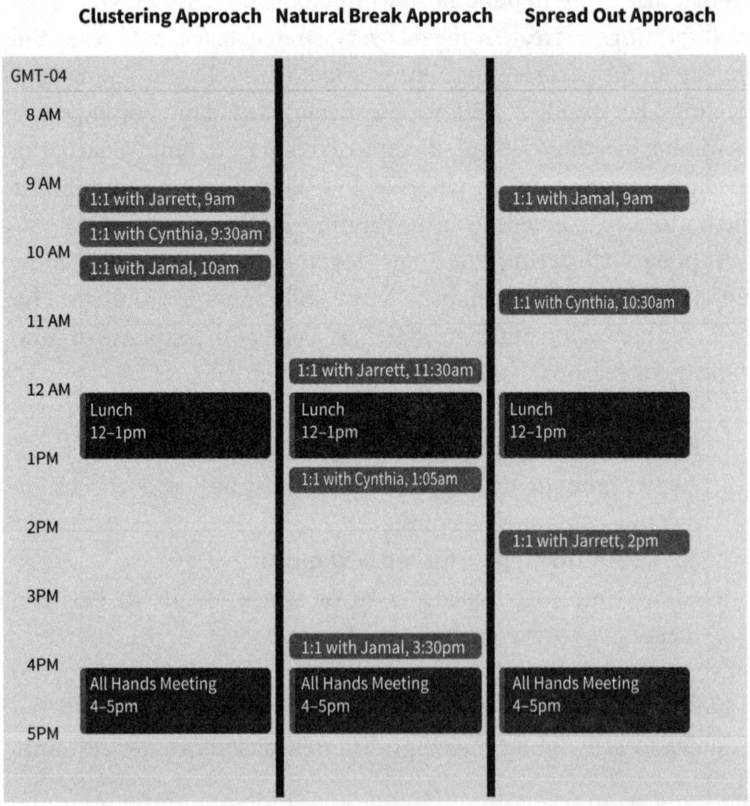

Overall, scheduling 1:1 meetings and managing your workload is your job. You have agency. Best practices recommend identifying time blocks for your 1:1s that work best for you and ideally allow you opportunities for flow and deep work. Then, allow team members to pick within those windows of time so they also have some agency to create their own opportunity for flow. To do this effectively, the time blocks shared with directs must be sufficiently large so that a choice that works for both parties can be made. Once these time blocks are set, lock in the scheduled times for say 6 months to a year to create consistency and to prevent a reoccurring scheduling dance.

There are also a host of apps and resources out there that can help you and your directs find meeting times that work with your schedules. For example, The Microsoft Teams meeting platform has a "scheduling assistant" feature, where others can view your availability and suggest times to meet that work with both schedules. In this case, you could block off designated time on your schedule that you want to protect (meeting-free time) to work on your own tasks. This block will show you as "busy" when others view your calendar. Then, any other free times on your schedule is fair game for directs to suggest a 1:1 meeting time.

Should I schedule all 1:1s on the same day? The research has yet to speak directly to this question. This is really a matter of personal preference. What we do know is that successful 1:1s require focus and energy—as does any meeting. Having 1:1s all on the same day can be a big ask for the leader if you have too many of them. But ultimately, that is up to you to decide.

Canceling 1:1s

One final topic to cover in this chapter, which is not often thought about, involves canceling 1:1s. 1:1s should only be canceled if you truly have no other option. 1:1s are an investment in your people and your team, thus should be held sacred. Even if you have business travel or can't make it to the office, it's best to find the time to meet via a phone call while on the road, at the airport, or between meetings. Granted, you will likely need to shorten the meeting time, and this is fine. But, in these and related circumstances, even just 5–10 minutes of 1:1 time can be productive and send a strong message of importance to your directs. Also, if it's a particularly tricky week, you can always try asynchronous methods like using a shared document where you and your direct can provide updates, comments, and thoughts. This can absolutely work, and it's often an underused approach by managers. This is not a 1:1 per se, but it serves to support the 1:1 process. If you must cancel because of some type of emergency, be sure to take the initiative and reschedule it right away. Ideally, you should reschedule for the same week or as soon as possible. In the case that you foresee a scheduling conflict emerging, move up the 1:1 meeting rather than moving it back as this conveys to your people that they are a high priority to you.

Can a team member cancel the 1:1? The answer is, of course, yes. However, you should monitor how often they cancel 1:1s to see if a pattern emerges. Repeated cancellations by team members may signal a problem. In cases like this, managers need to get a better understanding of what is at the root of these requests before deciding what to do with this information. Our initial research suggests—and this is very important—that often when a direct indicates the desire for fewer 1:1s, it is actually rooted in a quality/value concern and *not* a time concern. Namely, the best predictor I found in my research on the desire by the direct to reduce 1:1 meeting time was not how busy they were, but how well or poorly the manager ran the 1:1. For example, when the manager did not truly engage with what was on their directs' minds, fewer 1:1s were desired. See Chapter 13 on how to get feedback on your 1:1s.

Key Takeaways

- **Find a Scheduling Approach That Works for You.** While research suggests that clustering meetings tends to be most optimal to promote uninterrupted time, limit task-switching, and achieve greater flow, managers differ in whether they desire this approach. Scheduling is ultimately the role of the manager, so pick the schedule that aligns with your needs and preferences while also giving your directs some agency in this decision.

- **Understand That How Meetings Are Scheduled Can Affect You and Your Directs, and Plan Accordingly.** Build in microbreaks (such as shortening a 30-minute 1:1 to be 25 minutes) so you can digest information from the previous meeting and prepare for the next. Schedule 1:1s during natural transition times (like lunch) to limit task-switching and cognitive demands. Last, if you want to have all of your 1:1s on the same day, that is fine. But be cognizant of your meeting load and how that may affect you and your 1:1s.
- **Very Rarely Cancel 1:1s.** Doing so may be experienced by your direct that they are not a priority to you. If necessary (such as in the case of an emergency), reschedule the 1:1 immediately and near the original date. If you foresee that a 1:1 will have to be cancelled, reschedule the meeting before it was supposed to happen rather than after. In doing so, you signal to your team that their task and personal needs are important to you.

5
Shall We Take a Walk?

Where humans gather, matters. Namely, elements of the environment can influence emotions and behavior in meaningful ways. Take these research findings for example:

- Chess players made more errors when indoor air pollution was higher.[1]
- Performance decreased on the PSAT (a standardized college-entrance type exam) when taken in warmer rooms.[2]
- High-noise room environments negatively affected individuals' ability to form memories and induced feelings of fatigue.[3]
- Patients disclosed more information to their physicians in larger rooms as opposed to smaller rooms.[4]
- More creative problem-solving strategies were generated in rooms with high ceilings in comparison to rooms with lower ceilings.[5]
- My research on departmental staff meetings found that appropriate lighting, a size of the room that was not too big or too small for the number of attendees, and a comfortable temperature were all related to meeting satisfaction.[6]

Even the color of rooms has been investigated. Although contentious given the lack of conclusive data, yellow is thought to induce hunger. Guess what color McDonald's interior is?! Blue is thought to induce a calm and relaxing state. Therefore, if you want customers to linger at a tavern/pub/bar, blue may be the choice of ambiance so that customers order more drinks over a larger span of time. Although thinking of a room's color as causing hunger or calm feels like a bit of a reach, research is quite confident that color is associated with mood and subsequent decision-making to some extent.[7] The bottom line is that space is worth considering when organizing 1:1s. Each location brings with it both positives and negatives. There are a host of options to consider. This chapter is about *where* to conduct your 1:1s. Later, I will present data from directs and leaders on location suggestions they believe are optimal.

Locations for 1:1s

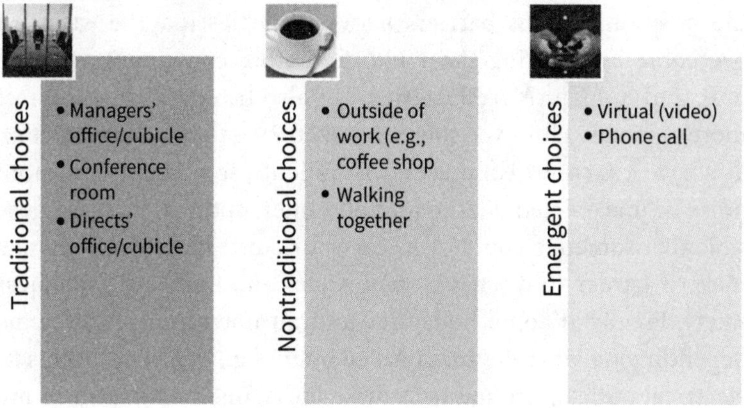
Traditional choices
• Managers' office/cubicle
• Conference room
• Directs' office/cubicle
Nontraditional choices
• Outside of work (e.g., coffee shop
• Walking together
Emergent choices
• Virtual (video)
• Phone call

Traditional Meeting Locations

Meeting in your office is a common and totally appropriate choice for 1:1s, assuming it is unshared and you can minimize distractions and disruptions. The direct's office is another fine option. There are many things I like about this option, including signaling this is a meeting for the direct. Plus, it provides the manager with a window of insight into the direct's workspace and organization (e.g., observe wall hangings, pictures, and the like to see what is important to your direct). However, scheduling a meeting in the direct's space can be experienced as a bit intrusive and assertive. Thus, a third option is a conference room. A conference room represents a neutral space, which I like. However, conference rooms can be tricky to schedule at times and may not have the files and access to computers that would best facilitate the meeting.

Nontraditional Meeting Locations

1:1s can certainly be held in a restaurant, coffee shop, or outside on a bench. When outside of the traditional office environment, the positional status barriers between parties may be easier to overcome by allowing the 1:1 to feel more conversational, natural, and human. A fresh setting can also be energizing and feel more personal. However, there are downsides to these settings too. You have less control of these environments, so there may be more noise or unexpected distractions and interruptions. It is also possible that someone could overhear your conversation, which may make it harder to discuss certain topics and build psychological safety. Finally, it could be harder to draft notes and action items depending on what the space has to offer (e.g., table size, access to electrical outlets). In line with these ideas, one respondent in my research noted:

> *One of the biggest values of the 1:1 is the ability to be frank with each other. So, I wouldn't want to have a 1:1 with them at a public location, or in a cubicle farm where others are right there.*

These downsides could certainly be mitigated by picking an outside location thoughtfully, so that privacy is assured, and picking a time where crowding is less of an issue. Plus, you can use your phone to write down/dictate notes rather than dragging along your laptop or a notebook. A quick internet search will yield a host of compelling voice-to-note apps that can be leveraged.

Psychological safety is a belief that one will not be punished for speaking up with ideas, raising questions or concerns, or making mistakes. Feelings of psychological safety are critical for transparent, honest, and meaningful 1:1s. This means creating an environment that makes your direct feel comfortable raising questions, voicing concerns, and sharing ideas without fear of repercussions. Keep this in mind when you are considering locations for your meetings. You do not want to compromise your direct's feelings of psychological safety, especially if the meeting agenda includes sensitive or private topics.

Taking a Walk

A number of leaders are big fans of the walking meeting. For example, in his biography, Steve Jobs references his passion for having serious conversations on long walks. Other examples are Mark Zuckerberg, Twitter cofounder Jack Dorsey, and former president Barack Obama. So, does research support the use of walking meetings? You bet. To start, it's good for you! The health benefits of walking include decreased risk of heart disease, improved weight control, lowered risk of certain types of cancer and dementia, lowered cholesterol, and increased bone and muscle strength. In addition to the physical health benefits, there are also mental health benefits, such as increased well-being. For example, in a study of walking meetings, results showed that after 90 days of leveraging walking meetings, participants reported increased energy and improved engagement.

Unsurprisingly, increased energy and engagement bodes well for meetings—it can even enhance focus and creativity. In fact, research on walking meetings found those that those that had them were 8.5% more likely to report high levels of engagement overerall with the job and reported being more creative at work.[8] Another study examining the link between walking and creativity showed that walking outside boosted creativity more than the other conditions they tested, such as creative exercises while sitting. Additionally, looking in the same direction while doing the same activity (walking) creates a collaborative feeling, as opposed to sitting across from one another and staring at each other. This can be particularly well-suited to when you have a difficult conversation. It makes the conversations feel less formal. Ultimately, research shows that walking is beneficial for both the mind and body and produces favorable outcomes related to job performance,[9] suggesting that taking your 1:1s outside for a walk can be beneficial.

There are also downsides to walking meetings to be mindful of. There can be distractions. You may run into people you know. Referencing notes and taking them can be difficult (although note-taking issues can be easily rectified with a voice-to-note app as mentioned earlier). Note, if your 1:1 is slated for more than 30 minutes, the walking time might be a bit much for some people. Relatedly, walking meetings are not a good fit for all people, given a physical challenge or disability, or just a dislike of walking and doing business at the same time. It also is weather-dependent. No one wants to walk in the rain or blistering cold (or sweltering hot) conditions. As such, if you do pursue this option, it is essential to ask your direct their preferences, and notify parties in advance so proper shoes can be worn. Plan a route so you finish the walk when the meeting is supposed to end. This route should also be relatively quiet and free of too many distractions—something that not all workplaces can provide. Finally, create a backup plan for the meeting if bad weather arises. One final thing to add: Walking meetings for your remote team members are also viable and should be considered. In this model, you schedule the 1:1 and then both hop on the phone as you take a walk. This feels different, keeps the blood flowing, and can work very well.

One final note about taking notes during walking meetings if you don't want to take them in real time on your phone: I suggest taking notes immediately following the 1:1. As soon as you return to your office, cubicle, or desk—jot down key takeaways from the 1:1. Have your direct do the same. Then, share your takeaways to ensure you are on the same page and nothing was forgotten or misconstrued.

Preference Data

I don't have data on which 1:1 location leads to the best outcomes, although I wish I did. I do, however, have data from managers and team members on location *preferences* that are quite telling and insightful. Here are the percentage of respondents who were favorable or unfavorable toward various location choices.

Location	Favorable	Unfavorable
Manager's office:	51%	19%
Directs office:	29%	35%
Conference room	52%	18%
Outside location (e.g., a coffee shop):	45%	29%
Taking a walk:	48%	31%

The highest-rated locations were the manager's office or a conference room. The direct's office was the lowest-rated location and is clearly not preferred by most. Interestingly, support for outside locations (e.g., coffee shop) and taking a walk (in person or over the phone) were bimodal. Namely, interest in these options was around 50%. However, around 30% of respondents rated those locations as unfavorable. Thus, some directs desired this approach while others felt the opposite. This speaks to the importance of communicating with each direct to understand their individual preferences regarding meeting location. It is worth noting that preferences for different locations were not tied to the gender, job level, or age of respondents.

Go Virtual

What do we know about virtual 1:1s—not a ton. First, let me note that thus far in my research I have found no meaningful consequences on effectiveness due to 1:1s being in person versus virtual. We did observe that a slight majority preferred to be in person for 1:1s (55%), but the level of comfort with virtual 1:1s was very high, indicating it doesn't seem to make a difference whether the 1:1 is virtual or in person. Here are some of the data collected about why respondents preferred in-person or virtual 1:1s, respectively:

Themes and Quotes from Those Who Prefer In-Person 1:1s

Themes from those who prefer in-person 1:1s	Evidence (quotes)
Nonverbal communication is richer/more personal/private	"*Face to face is more personal, permits better communication, allows nonverbal communication.*"
Easier to focus & engage/fewer distractions than virtual meetings	"*Easier to get distracted by emails, etc. when it is virtual. [1:1s] seem more focused when in person.*"
Easier to share information and documents	"*Easier to share nondigital information*"
Helps establish rapport/relationship building	"*This is almost 50/50 for me, but when in person we have more ability to balance warmth with business.*" "*It's easier to build rapport and have little side observations and conversations that humanize us to each other in person. You can do that virtually, but it requires more active work and attention, which most managers typically don't make time for.*"

Themes and Quotes from Those Who Prefer Virtual 1:1s

Themes from those who prefer virtual 1:1s	Evidence (quotes)
Easier to share documents	*"My work is almost exclusively done on the computer, so it is helpful to share screens to identify folders on the shared drive and review files that I have questions about."*
Preference for remote work in general/live far away from other meeting attendees	*"I prefer to work from home. Our 1:1 meetings have been very productive in this virtual setting. Face-to-face is good too, I just prefer to work virtually in general."* *"In person is not feasible in my global org. I generally am not located in the same state as my manager."*
More efficient/to the point	*"More time efficient/comfy."*
Easier for introverts to engage	*"I am honestly more introverted, and it allows me to speak more freely when I am on camera versus being in person. I hold back more when I'm in person."*

I do want to add, there were comments that talked about how preferences for virtual vs. face-to-face are dependent on the nature of the conversation and what is being covered, with the suggestion that deeper and more substantive issues may be better suited for in-person conversations. Also, there were some junior employees who felt the in-person facetime could be helpful for their career advancement and development. Overall, virtual 1:1s have many positives. It may not be ideal for all situations, but they may be the only option for many. Based on the data, if readily possible, do face-to-face for your 1:1s. But, if not possible, virtual is a very reasonable option. Finally, it is important to point out that it is not necessarily an either-or situation as this respondent's comment notes:

> *I'd prefer a mix of virtual in some kind of ratio of 5–1 where mostly we connect virtually as both of us travel and are very busy, so they happen more often. Having an occasional lunch/walk/coffee just brings us to more personal topics or random thoughts that don't emerge in a more efficient/focused virtual meeting.*

As you consider virtual 1:1s, here are 10 general tips on how to get the most out of virtual interactions in general.

Best Practices for Virtual 1:1s	
1. Test your technology before hand to avoid hiccups	6. Angle your camera level on your face
2. Avoid multitasking to stay focused	7. Turn off "self-view" on your video platform for a more natural conversation
3. Have your camera/video on to create more presence.	8. Ensure reliable internet
4. Have good lighting to pick up on nonverbals	9. Limit distractions
5. Consider using your actual background (when possible) to come across more natural	10. Use virtual tools like a whiteboard to promote engagement and documentation

Get Input

In looking at these data on meeting location preferences, there is clear variability in the desires for or against 1:1s being in different locations and going virtual. Thus, a conversation is needed in advance to gauge where your direct feels most comfortable for their

1:1s. They know what they like, don't like, or perhaps they just don't care. Asking for preferences also helps communicate that the meeting is being designed for the direct to be comfortable. The key is picking a location where everyone can feel at ease, present, psychologically safe, and free of distractions to fully engage in the meetings. Furthermore, 1:1s don't have to be in the same place every time. And you don't have to change location every time either. But we do know that it is often the case that we can easily fall into ruts where we repeat practices over time almost mechanically. Sometimes it helps to mix things up by changing meeting locations to keep 1:1s feeling fresh.

Key Takeaways

- **Space Matters.** Where you meet can affect how productive 1:1s are. Ensure that wherever you decide to have your 1:1s, the space is conducive to having an effective meeting. Privacy, air quality, room temperature, noise levels, potential distractions, and even the weather (during walking meetings) can negatively impact your 1:1s.
- **Location Options Exist.** There are both traditional and nontraditional location choices for 1:1s. Based on the research, traditional choices, like a manager's office or a private conference room, are great options. However, nontraditional locations exist too. Consider going for a walking 1:1 meeting or heading to the nearest coffee shop. Just be mindful of the pros and cons of each location. Relatedly, virtual 1:1s are another great option that most employees are very open too.
- **Find What Works, but also Switch Things Up at Times.** Discuss with your direct reports what works for you both. Some directs may prefer one location, while others will have better 1:1s in a different location. The key is to figure out the sweet spot. Regardless, consider switching the location up from time to time. Doing so keeps things fresh and prevent 1:1s from becoming stale.

6

Is a Good "How Are You" Enough?

I don't mind answering thoughtful questions.
But I'm not thrilled about answering questions like,
"If you were being mugged, and you had a lightsaber in one pocket
and a whip in the other, which would you use?"

— Harrison Ford

This chapter is about identifying what should be talked about and asked in 1:1s to spur rich, meaningful conversations. There are many choices to consider. Going back to the chapter title, a good "How are you?" or "How is life?" can indeed bring forward issues and topics of great importance. Phrases like these can provoke all kinds of good dialogue, especially if the direct perceives the questions as being genuine and sincere. However, the main problem with questions like the above are they typically elicit quick, socially engrained answers ("fine," "pretty good," and "great"). They just don't tend to inspire much thought and reflection. There is an intriguing tweak however, grounded in research,[1] that can make a general check-in question like this yield deeper insights. Here is what it looks like.

You Ask: "Take a moment and think about what is going on in life and at work—based on that, how are things for you?" or "Taking into consideration everything going on for you at the moment, how are you showing up today?" The twist, the direct has to answer using either a traffic light system or 10-point rating scale. With regard to the former, "green" means all is good, they are happy, and they are thriving. "Yellow" means things are generally okay, but there are some issues and stress; they are still getting by, but not easily. "Red" suggests directs have meaningful concerns, challenges, and worries that need to be addressed. An alternative approach is to have the direct answer on a 10-point response scale from 0 very poorly to 10 very good. In both cases you will tend to inspire more thought and the response you get back will give you something to explore. For example, "tell me more, why you feeling like a 'yellow' today or like a '6' today, what's going on?" The additional candor and depth is key to a great 1:1.

So, yes, a good sincere "How are you?" is indeed at the core of an excellent 1:1. But, it won't allow us to reach the full potential of 1:1s. Let's consider additional options to diversify the meeting and to cover more meaningful topics. To help with this effort, I interviewed over 250 employees and asked them two questions about what they see as the best questions to ask. All responses were content analyzed, and the top five themes were revealed. Here are the results:

What are the best questions a manager should ask during a 1:1?	**What are the best questions a direct report should ask during a 1:1?**
How can I help you?	How can I help you?
How are you doing?/What is going well?	How am I doing?/What feedback do you have for me around X?
What do you need from me?	What can I do for you? How can I support you?
How can I support you?/What resources can I provide?	What should I be prioritizing?
What barriers/roadblocks/challenges are you facing? What is not going well?	How might I advance my career? How can I improve/grow/develop/do better?

The above questions are great. They push on a larger breadth of topics, and even more importantly, they bring in help/support/

counsel into the conversation. There is a greater range of questions to consider. This chapter lays out even more questions that can be discussed in 1:1s.

Obviously, you can only ask so many questions during any single 1:1. However, rotating different questions periodically in creates interesting and well-rounded conversations across time and 1:1s. Some questions may feel right for you and your relationship with your direct, while others may not, and that is totally fine. Think of the following examples as just a giant menu of options to consider. Moreover, I added a list of special questions for remote employees that can be found in the tools shared at the end of this book section.

With some exceptions, the questions are generally framed as things you, as a manager, can ask. But certainly, most of these questions can be asked by the directs to you either as-is or with a little tweaking if they so desire. Let me share an example to illustrate:

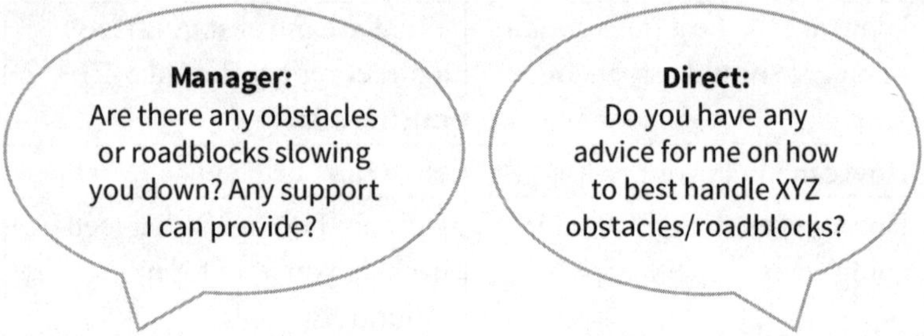
Manager:
Are there any obstacles or roadblocks slowing you down? Any support I can provide?
Direct:
Do you have any advice for me on how to best handle XYZ obstacles/roadblocks?

Categories of Questions

Combining questions I curated in my research, along with an extensive literature review, six overarching, but highly interconnected, categories of questions emerged. As noted earlier, the ideal is to sample questions across categories to create rich and multifaceted conversations over time.

Relationship Building

Building a personal and professional relationship requires the parties to get to know one another, to discover commonalities, and to explore differences. The first part for this is learning about the other party as a person—who they are outside of work. This should be a gradual process because trust and comfort need time to build, which makes disclosure easier to do. However, stay within your direct's comfort zone every step of the way. The second part is learning about the work-related preferences of your direct.

Part 1: Getting to Know Your Direct on a More Personal Level

- What is something you are excited about right now, outside of work?
- What are some of your favorite things to do to relax?

- What are you watching, reading or listening to these days (podcasts/books/music/movies)?
- What is your favorite way to spend a day off?
- Where is the next place on your bucket list to travel to?
- How are things going outside of work for you?
- Is there anything that you'd like to know about me?

Part 2: Getting to Know One Another's Work-Related Preferences

- Think about the best manager you've ever had, what did you like about them?
- How do you like and dislike being managed?
- How do you like to organize and/or structure your day?
- What makes you feel appreciated when you've done a good job?
- What motivates you at work?
- What do you see as your best strengths?
- What kind of a workplace would help you be the happiest version of you?
- What are your biggest pet peeves in the workplace that I should be aware of?
- What should I know about you that would best help me be most useful and supportive of you?

Engagement

Fostering and maintaining employee engagement is a key role for any leader. To do so, it is important to understand how the team member feels about their job, their role, their day-to-day tasks, what leads them to stay, and what would drive them out the door.

Part 1: Day-to-Day

- What part of your job do you not enjoy? What do you enjoy most?
- Since you started this role, has it been what you expected? Any good or bad surprises?

- Do you derive meaning from your work? If not, what changes could help?
- Are there any aspects of your job that you wish you could eliminate so you could focus on more important/rewarding responsibilities?
- Do you feel good about your work/life balance? Is there anything I can do to help with that?

Part 2: Retention

- What could make this job and/or organization more compelling to you so that you would want to stay long-term?
- What aspects of this job and/or organization might tempt you to leave?
- Do you feel like this organization is a place you can grow, develop, and thrive?
- What aspect of another job or organization might tempt you to go with them?
- What would a plan look like to keep you happy and thriving here?

When asking questions around retention and improving the work environment for your directs, be aware that some of their suggestions may be out of your control. For example, if your direct would like to work from home this might not be feasible or even your call to make. Your direct could then become frustrated if their suggestions aren't implemented. To avoid this, do not overpromise. Make a good effort to carry out their hopes. Follow up as needed to explain what you can and can't do and why.

Check-In

This category is about understanding key work activities, sharing important updates, following up on items, and perhaps most importantly, making sure there is alignment in priorities between the direct and you.

- What's top of your mind?
- Any updates on the action items from our last 1:1?
- What are you currently working on that perhaps I don't know about, but should?
- Let's review the major job/work/goal/performance metrics we are tracking. How are things going? What help/support can I provide?
- What has gone well/not so well workwise for you over the last X weeks?
- What are your priorities over the next X days? What can we do to help you with this?
- One thing we talked about at your last performance review/coaching discussion was X. How's that going?

When you are asking some of the above questions, be sure not to come across as micromanaging. You don't want your direct to leave the 1:1 feeling like you are trying to control every minor detail of their work. Micromanagement can strain your relationship, reduce engagement, compromise morale, and decrease productivity. To avoid this, readily ask questions from other buckets. In other words, try not to make one meeting solely focused on asking check-in questions.

Productivity/Challenges

One of the key purposes of a 1:1 is the offering of help and support—helping the direct to thrive. To do so, you must understand the challenges your direct is experiencing. These challenges can emerge from specific work assignments, from the team itself, or from the directs of your direct report.

Part 1: Addressing Roadblocks, Obstacles, or Concerns

- What is slowing you down or blocking you? What help/support can I provide?

- Are your roles and responsibilities clear? Anything I can clarify?
- Last time we spoke you said X was a challenge for you, how is that going?
- We all have things that feel like they waste our time at work. What are yours?
- How can I best set you up for success?

Part 2: Assessing Perceptions of Your Team

- How is our team culture? What do you see as opportunities for improvement?
- Are team members communicating readily with one another?
- Do you feel like a valued member of the team?
- Do you feel we have an inclusive team environment?
- Any support/help the team needs from me, in your opinion?

Part 3: How Things Are Going with the Direct Reports of Your Directs (If Applicable)

- How are things with your team members/directs?
- Are any stars emerging? Any problems with team members you want to talk about?
- Are there any flight risks among your best performers?
- Anything I can do to support you in your efforts to manage your team?
- Anything you think would be helpful for me to know about regarding your team?
- Is there anyone you think it would be helpful for me to meet with?

Giving/Receiving Feedback

1:1s are an ideal opportunity to communicate and share feedback in a personal, directed, and deep manner. At the heart of this is providing feedback (discussed extensively later in Section 2 of the book) and gathering feedback about your role as manager, your meetings, and the organization more broadly.

Part 1: Giving Feedback to Directs

- Do I give you enough feedback? Is my feedback helpful? If not, how can I improve to help you succeed?
- Where can I provide more feedback/coaching? Think about a work activity or a skill you are working on where you would like more feedback.
- What feedback can I share with you today that could be helpful—any particular projects, tasks, skills that you'd like feedback on now?
- Do you feel like I acknowledge/recognize the positive work that you do?

Part 2: Organizational Communication to a Team Member

- Do you have any questions about (*insert something going on at the company/team*)?
- What are your thoughts/reaction to (*insert something going on at the company/team)?*
- I wanted to tell you about (*insert something going on at the company/team*) to gather your thoughts and see if you had any questions.

Part 3: Receiving Feedback about Your Performance as a Manager

- I want to be the best manger I can be. How can I improve on (*insert different topics—delegation, communication, team dynamics, prioritization, etc.*)?
- Would you like more/less direction from me?
- In your opinion, what do you think I am doing particularly well as your manager and not so well?

- Anything you think I should know about (*insert a topic—the team, the job, the organization, etc.*)?
- Anything I can be doing differently to help you or other team members?
- If you were coaching me to be the best leader I could be, what advice would you give me?

Part 4: Receiving Feedback about Your Meetings

- Do you feel like we have too many/too few meetings? Any meetings you think we can cancel, change, or do differently?
- What are your thoughts on our team meetings? How can we make them more productive?
- Are our 1:1 meetings working for you? What needs to start, stop, and continue?
- What do you think went well and not so well during meeting X last week?

Part 5: Receiving Feedback about the Company/Team

- In your opinion, what is the #1 opportunity for our company/team?
- What are our biggest blind spots, risks, or problems as a company/team?
- If you were the CEO, what would you change today?
- What are your most and least favorite parts of our culture as an organization/team?

Development, Growth, and Career Questions

This section is all about looking ahead. It is about exploring future paths and working to get there. It moves beyond day-to-day work and focuses more on the direct's long-term possibilities and hopes for the future.

- Where do you expect yourself to be career-wise in 5–10 years?
- Tell me about your long-term goals. How can I best help you reach them?
- What can you do and what can I do to help you achieve your aspirations?
- Do you feel you are making progress on the long-term goals you have set for yourself?
- What are two or three new sets of knowledge/skills you'd like to learn in this job?
- Is there something that is not a part of your present role that you want to be doing?
- Is there someone within the company (or outside) that you'd like to learn from?
- What progress have you made on your career goals this month?
- Are there other parts of the business you would like to learn more about or get connected with in some way?
- What type of role/job do you aspire to have after this one?

The questions above are stated generically, but they clearly can—and often should—be made more specific to the job or role of your direct. I encourage you to tailor and tweak the questions to feel more relevant to you and your direct, and in your voice.

Final Notes and Considerations

With a quick Google search, you can find additional questions for 1:1s. The key is finding questions that you feel good about and that can inspire fruitful conversations. Avoid questions that just result in a team member reciting their contributions or questions that have you come across as controlling/micromanaging (e.g., "What did you do this week?"). I inserted a checklist of common mistakes for 1:1 questions in the tools area following this book section.

Some questions may be asked more frequently (e.g., questions from the "Check-In" category) as they are likely affecting the day-to-day experience of work, while others can be addressed regularly, but not weekly or biweekly, as they focus more on the future (e.g., "Development, Growth, and Career" questions). Plan to sample the questions broadly over time to keep the 1:1s well-rounded and stimulating for all, while being mindful in the process.

Certain questions could be context-specific, as well. For example, if this is your first 1:1 with a team member, sample heavily from the "Getting to Know Each Other" and the "Development, Growth, and Career" categories. Alternatively, if you want the 1:1 to focus on retaining a direct who may seem like they are a flight risk, you can sample heavily from the "Development, Growth, and Career" as well as "Retention" and "Check-In" categories.

I cannot stress enough that there is not a magic formula to 1:1s, including what questions are asked. You must pick what works for you, your direct, and your relationship with them. Basically, find the best questions through trial and error that fit the relationship and levels of comfort and trust. And remember, you are your direct's manager—not their therapist. With that said, if needed, you can always make a referral to HR, an employee assistance professional, and/or an external coach. Be sure to respect your boundaries and the boundaries of the relationship.

Finally and perhaps most importantly, the key to asking questions that generate meaningful conversations is sincerity and genuine interest in their responses—listening carefully, exploring what is shared, and providing support where you can. Without this, even the best questions asked will fail. In Chapter 9, I discuss how to effectively probe and follow up on answers shared by your direct.

Key Takeaways

- **"How Are You?" Is Not Enough.** Asking a question like this is not thought-provoking or helpful in eliciting meaningful conversations. While it is okay to ask—especially in novel ways like the traffic light system—it should not be the driving question of your 1:1s.

- **So Many Good Questions to Consider.** Ask more nuanced questions to create high-quality dialogue in your 1:1s. Sample thoughtfully from the six categories forwarded: 1) Relationship-Building, 2) Engagement, 3) Check-In, 4) Productivity/ Challenges, 5) Giving/Receiving Feedback, and 6) Development, Growth, and Career. It may be overwhelming to decide what questions to use in your 1:1s, given how many options are available. Take a step back, think of what will work for your situation and your direct, and tailor questions accordingly. This will take some prep work for you, but will boost the effectiveness of your 1:1 conversations and demonstrate your care, thoughtfulness, and support to your directs.
- **Switch Up the Questions You Ask.** The question options shared are a great way to provide depth and range to your 1:1 conversations. Avoid asking questions from just one category. Also, make sure to switch up the specific questions you ask over time. This will keep your 1:1s fresh and engaging, while covering a variety of topics to support your direct, their work/needs, and your relationship with them.

7

Do These Meetings Need an Agenda?

> *The most important criterion governing matters to be talked about is that they be issues that preoccupy and nag the subordinate.*
>
> Andy Grove, Former CEO and Co-Founder Intel

I have found the topic of whether agendas are useful in a 1:1 to be quite a divisive question among managers, with some seeing them as very important and others seeing them as burdensome and unnecessary. What do you think? Agenda or no agenda?

Data exist to help navigate this question, and they may surprise you. Having an agenda, which appears to happen around 50% of the time based on my data, created in advance or even at the beginning of the meeting itself, was indeed associated with more positive ratings of 1:1 meeting value. Interestingly, who created the agenda—the direct, their manager, or both—appears to be the key factor to consider. Namely, 1:1 value ratings were highest when the agenda was created jointly or by the direct only, and lowest when the agenda was created solely by the manager. These findings certainly align with the notion that 1:1s are ultimately a meeting for the team member. Furthermore, what is clear in my interviews with both managers and team members is that people were not looking for an extensive or formal agenda. Instead, they were just looking for some type of a priori plan. A plan, even if informal and communicated at the beginning of the meeting, serves to prime the conversation and create focus. Putting this together, the data suggest that agendas are helpful, but do not need to be detailed or highly structured for 1:1s to be effective. Instead, agendas should be created in a way to engage strongly with the direct and to map out some type of path forward, ideally in advance, to make your 1:1 meeting time intentional and meaningful.

Starting Agenda Items

The first item on the agenda should be an easy conversation starter. Don't get straight to business. Taking five minutes to build rapport and learn what is going on with your directs communicates that you care and are interested in the team member as a person. If the direct is comfortable, out-of-work content can absolutely be discussed (keep it professional of course). Life happens, and it affects work. For example, in one story that came up in my interviews, the direct discussed the anxiety they were feeling around providing eldercare. This led to the manager helping the team member tweak their work schedule to decrease time conflicts, relieving a lot of stress for the direct. While success stories like this can happen, follow your direct's lead on how personal they want to get. This interview quote from an executive at Boston Beer, makers of Sam Adams, captures well what the first agenda items should be: *"A key piece of a 1:1 is truly to get to know your direct, what is their personal story, and of great relevance, what drives them. This allows you to truly connect with your people. This connection is so important."*

After rapport-building, ask about something linked to the last 1:1 meeting (following up on a problem, asking how X worked out, etc.). This sends a strong message that you take these meetings seriously, you were listening carefully at the last meeting, and that the 1:1s connect with and build off one another. This can be very motivating to the team member and reflects positively on you. It is important to note that you don't want to rehash the entirety of the last meeting. That is not the goal. This is just a quick hit. With that said, if the direct wants to revisit past agenda items, that is certainly fine and appropriate.

The next starting agenda item can focus on you recognizing wins and expressing appreciation and gratitude toward your direct. These kind words create comfort, connection, and feelings of safety, and can help the conversation build forward momentum. Putting this all together, the first agenda items should go as the following:

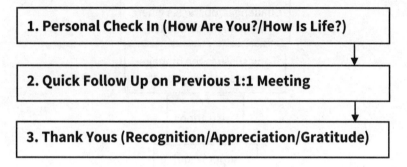

1. Personal Check In (How Are You?/How Is Life?)

↓

2. Quick Follow Up on Previous 1:1 Meeting

↓

3. Thank Yous (Recognition/Appreciation/Gratitude)

Agenda Building Models for the Core of the Meeting: The Two Most Common Approaches

The Listing Approach to Agendas

1:1 meeting agendas can be built in many ways. Yet, two approaches emerged most frequently in my interviews. Both are lightweight and flexible. The simplest agenda-building model for the core of the 1:1, receiving many positive reviews, is called the **listing approach.** It involves you and the direct separately creating a list of topics to discuss. Then, at the meeting, the direct works through their list first, followed by you working through your list. To better understand this approach, I will provide more details, broken by role in the 1:1.

Team Member Role. Encourage your direct to avoid just creating a laundry list of agenda items. Instead, their list should contain key topics and key priorities based on their current needs. The list should integrate tactical work issues, as well as longer-horizon issues, such as career development. The list should focus on the good, the bad, and the ugly in the present, but also address what matters down the road.

To prompt ideas, you can tell the direct to reflect on a range of topics as you don't want this to just be an update meeting (more on that later):

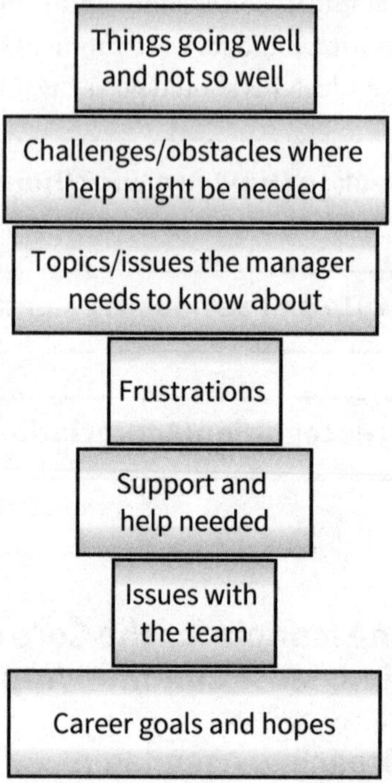
Things going well and not so well
Challenges/obstacles where help might be needed
Topics/issues the manager needs to know about
Frustrations
Support and help needed
Issues with the team
Career goals and hopes

This process does not necessarily come naturally to all. It is okay if the manager shares potential items or suggested topics with the team member, especially in the early 1:1s. The suggestions can be banal items (e.g., would love to hear more about what happened with customer X) or even more vexing ones (e.g., I know you have been really frustrated with X, I would like to follow up on it) to better set the stage on what **could** be discussed. All this needs to be framed as *potential* topics for your direct to consider. You don't want the direct to feel like the meeting is about your needs, instead of their own. Somewhat related to this, a best practice for you and the team member is to keep a paper or virtual log over the course of your 1:1s of potential topics/issues that have been or could be discussed. This serves to enhance recall and helps mitigate a recency bias when creating agendas. Overall, there is tremendous variability in what the list can look like given the diversity of a direct's needs.

Manager Role. You most likely have a list of topics you'd like to discuss too. Your list may contain time-sensitive topics or longer-range topics. However, the main focus of the 1:1 should be on your direct's agenda topics. Still, a good way to generate a list is to consider the following:

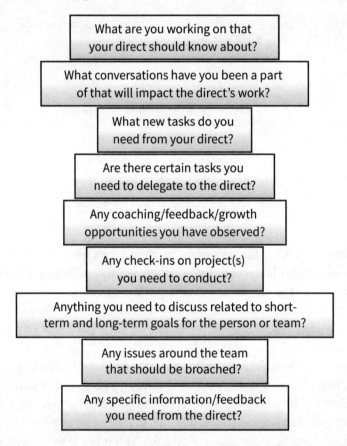

- What are you working on that your direct should know about?
- What conversations have you been a part of that will impact the direct's work?
- What new tasks do you need from your direct?
- Are there certain tasks you need to delegate to the direct?
- Any coaching/feedback/growth opportunities you have observed?
- Any check-ins on project(s) you need to conduct?
- Anything you need to discuss related to short-term and long-term goals for the person or team?
- Any issues around the team that should be broached?
- Any specific information/feedback you need from the direct?

While direct reports do not need to submit their agenda list in advance, I do think it is helpful for you to share your agenda or some of your agenda items in advance when relevant and possible. This can be 24–48 hours in advance, or even less if necessary. This can all be done with some bullet points. The goal in sharing this list is to prevent surprises in the meeting and hopefully allay some anxiety of the direct going into the 1:1. Here is what a sample email could look like:

Agenda List for Our 1:1 on Wednesday _ ⤢ ×

Enrica@company.com

Agenda List for Our 1:1 on Wednesday

Dear Enrica,

I am looking forward to our 1:1 on Wednesday. After we go through your agenda items, I'd like to cover the following - if we have time:

- Review a process change in our customer tracking system and answer any questions you may have.
- Discuss updates on the training project. If you could show me what you have so I can share some feedback, that would be great.
- Share with you some skills and techniques for dealing with difficult customers.
- I also would love to hear about how your trip up North went!

I look forward to seeing you and working through your list of items.

Thanks,
Gloria
The Manager

Both Parties. At the start of the meeting, take a few minutes to review each individual agenda list, and then negotiate a final set of topics to discuss. In the process of discussing initial lists, the parties may remove some items or push them to another meeting. That is fine. Often, lists are usually quite aligned. When they are not aligned, that provides meaningful information as well. In most all 1:1s, the direct's items should come first. If there is not time for all your topics, that is okay. You can always follow up later or schedule another 1:1 before your next one is scheduled to cover your topics if time sensitive. With that said, you typically will have moments to intersperse some of your ideas during the team member's discussion of their list. This is fine if your topics fit nicely into the conversation rhythm, and you are not forcing them. Be careful that your list does not hijack the meeting, however.

If you pursue this listing agenda approach, the core agenda items would be:

1. Discuss both lists and agree on what to cover (topics from each list can be included if helpful).

2. Go through direct's list of key topics.
3. Go through your list of key topics (as time allows).

Some managers and directs actual do #1 in advance of the meeting via asynchronous communication to allow for more time for #2 and #3 during the meeting itself.

A Second Approach: The Core Question Approach to Agendas

The core question approach came up quite frequently in my interviews, although the listing approach was most popular. In the core question approach, managers organize the 1:1 by listing a set of simple questions that represent the core of the agenda. The direct then answers the questions however they want and need. Thus, directs are really the ones controlling the content of the agenda and where the meeting will go. You, as the manager, are just providing the broad structure by prompting answers via general questions. Below are the core questions that came up quite frequently in my conversations:

1. Any problems/concerns/obstacles/challenges you would like to talk through?
2. What are your current priorities?
3. What is going well and not so well?
4. What do I need to know about/better understand?
5. Anything I can help you with or support you with or more on?
6. Anything else you want to talk about—think present, think future, think big picture and think small picture?

The team member knows about these questions in advance, so they are prepared to respond. Sometimes the direct might even answer the questions before the meeting via a shared document. The above were common core questions, but you can insert other core questions (see Chapter 6) that rotate across time, of course. If you do change core questions, just communicate questions all in advance so the direct is not blindsided and also can prepare if they choose.

After the core questions are discussed, the second part of the meeting is about you sharing your list of topics to discuss. Again, just as like the listing approach mentioned above, you may have natural and unforced moments to intersperse your issues during the direct's remarks. Just remember to prioritize your direct and their needs first and foremost.

The key caution in this approach as well as the listing approach to core agenda creation is that they tend to privilege immediate tactical issues and firefighting rather than longer-horizon issues such as career development. This is problematic because we don't want 1:1s to just fall into a status update trap. Before sharing solutions to the status trap, let me unpack what I mean by this in more detail.

Status Update Trap

The status update trap is when 1:1s take on a highly tactical, short-term orientation focusing on project updates and timelines. When this is the case, it becomes difficult to build rapport and trust. In fact, when conversations don't address issues such as growth and development, you might unintentionally be disengaging your direct reports as these issues are clearly important to their overall employee experience. More broadly, the full potential of 1:1s will go unrealized. Here is a great quote from an executive from Warner Brothers that really highlights this issue: "*Yes, 1:1s should get tactical, but you really want to be strategic. Namely, it should not just be a laundry list of items I am working on. That can be handled by other mechanisms. What you really want is depth and connection. 1:1s have to be much more than just status updates. They are about creating deep connections and rapport while also discussing non-task-related topics like development, strategic initiatives, and alignment for staying in sync.*"

Strategies for Preventing the Status Update Trap

While it is easy to fall into the status update trap, there are certainly ways to avoid it. In the following paragraphs I highlight three approaches for creating balanced 1:1s that help to prevent this trap.

Strategy 1: The Dedicated Minutes Approach

One way to avoid the status update trap is to religiously dedicate 5–15 minutes at every meeting to something nontactical and future oriented. For example, ask your direct a set of questions about career planning goals or developmental opportunities. These dedicated minutes can be labeled as the "futures" section of the 1:1 agenda.

Date of 1:1	Percentage of Time Discussing Short-Term Issues	Percentage of Time Discussing Long-Term Issues - Futures
January 2	70%	30%
January 9	70%	30%
January 16	70%	30%
January 23	70%	30%
January 30	70%	30%

You can rotate different longer-horizon topics in and out. To aid in this effort, one practice is to draft and share a plan for the futures section for say your next four 1:1s with a team member. While this is a tentative plan and can certainly change, it helps ensure that the meetings cover a range of topics over time. This approach also mitigates the risk of 1:1s falling into a predicable or stale pattern. I am not suggesting that 1:1s cannot have overlapping topics or reintroduce the same topics from time to time. Rather, I want to ensure coverage of a full range of topics and questions over time. Here is an example of this in practice from one manager:

Strategy 2: The Dedicated Meetings Approach

A second strategy is to dedicate every fourth or so 1:1 meeting (depending on your cadence) to primarily address longer-horizon topics. Be sure to periodically switch up the long-term topics of discussion, too. This approach elevates the discussion of long-term topics and assures that they happen. Here what this looks like:

Date of 1:1	Percentage of Time Discussing Short-Term Issues	Percentage of Time Discussing Long-Term Issues -- Futures
January 2	90%	10%
January 9	90%	10%
January 16	90%	10%
January 23	10%	90%
January 30	90%	10%

Strategy 3: The Template Approach

Consider the use of a formal meeting template that covers both short-term and long-term content. The template can provide structure to assure that 1:1s are balanced and comprehensive. I put a sample template in the tools section of this book to use and alter as desired. I know of no research that examines the effects of using meeting templates on 1:1 quality. And based on the surveys I have conducted; template usage is not all that high perhaps due to the large amount of structure it imposes. But it is something to consider and is clearly good for promoting coverage of topics and fostering consistency across people and time. There was one template practice, however, that came up in my interviews that intrigued me. After drafting a template, the manager sent it to each direct in advance of the meeting and asked them to tailor/alter the template to best meet their needs in future 1:1s. The template was also made into shared Google Docs (one for each direct). This way, updates could be made asynchronously between meetings for both parties to see. The shared document can also serve as a to-do list of sorts for action items as well as meeting notes/minutes.

Overall, be sensitive to the status update trap. Try different techniques to prevent falling victim to the trap so you and your direct can get the most out of 1:1s and reap their full value.

Should We Track Metrics as Part of the Agenda?

Performance, productivity, customer satisfaction, production errors, and other metrics can be tracked in 1:1s as an agenda item. In my work, I did not find that tracking metrics related to more positive perceptions of 1:1 effectiveness. I did ask managers and directs, "Do you think tracking metrics in 1:1s is a good approach?" Roughly 40% said yes, while the majority (60%) said no. Here were some of the comments made for each:

Those that said Yes (40%):	Those that said No (60%):
Tracking metrics removes ambiguity and prepares us to take future action.	*Metrics can be tracked with technology thus doing in a 1:1 isn't necessary; it is a waste of valuable time.*
Tracking metrics or milestones can help to keep expectations aligned.	*It tries to quantify things that are often hard to quantify or doesn't take important context into consideration. It also puts employees on the spot and reinforces harmful power dynamics. Furthermore, I don't impact them as much as the org thinks I do.*

Those that said Yes (40%):	Those that said No (60%):
Reduces surprises if things are going better or worse than planned.	*There are other mechanisms for that. I'm fine with using 1:1 time to dig into the why behind the metric though, especially if I need guidance on how to turn things around.*
I need the reality check. Am I delivering as promised? Not how hard did I try or what were the circumstances, but did I deliver in spite of the circumstances—that is the value I add.	*Metrics focus on things related primarily to revenue generation, which is good for the company to track in aggregate, but at an individual level tends to feel like micromanaging. Additionally, they tend to ignore "soft skill" impacts that are not well-measured through metrics.*
What gets measured gets done. What gets reviewed gets done correctly. What's important to my boss fascinates me.	*It makes the meetings too tactical and less focused on growth/development.*

Let me share one more piece of interesting data around metrics. Respondents were asked, "How often should metrics be examined in 1:1s?" Here were their responses:

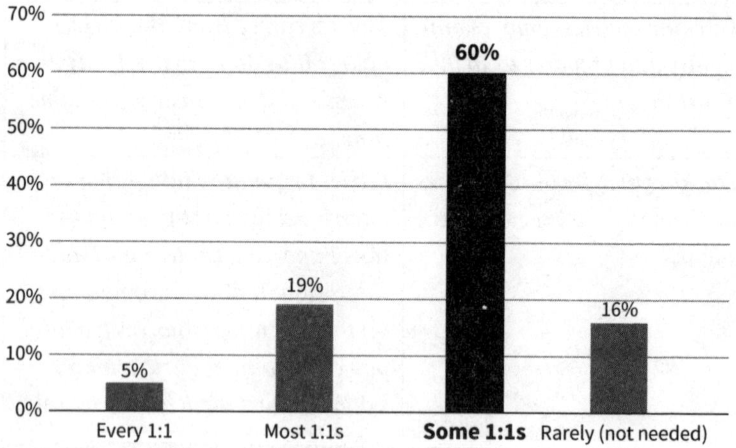

My takeaways from all the above data are that if metrics fit well with the job (e.g., sales role), track them in some (but not all) 1:1s. Tracking metrics can be insightful and useful at times, but they are not synonymous with the purpose of 1:1s. Most importantly, it is absolutely key to go underneath the metrics: the "why." This then leads to a discussion of how to achieve success with the metrics, barriers to success, and support needed for success; this is what the 1:1 should really be about. Additionally, remember that feedback should acknowledge effort exerted rather than just results, given that moving the dial on metrics is often impacted by the broader organizational and environmental context, not just the team member's direct performance.

Bottom line, remember the sage teachings of Ken Blanchard and Garry Ridge, "Your job as a manager is to help your people get an 'A,' not just monitor their grades."[1] You can still hold an employee accountable if they aren't performing at their best, but rather than using 1:1s as a time for judgment and evaluation, focus on elevating success and what actions and support can improve their metrics and future performance.

Closing Out the Agenda

Besides closing with gratitude, appreciation, and affirming content, the last agenda item should be a recap: "What are the next steps for each of us?" Make it clear what the expectations are for action items and their respective timelines. This will be discussed more later in the book.

Ten Final Notes About Agendas

1. Try Different Agenda Approaches
    - See what works best for you and team members. There is not one right path here. Ask for feedback to get it all right, which may change over time.

2. Adjust Agenda Approaches to Different Directs
   - There's no need to have the same agenda approach for all direct reports. Different people may need different things from you. Consult with each direct to identify the best way to carry out the agenda process for them. And remember, agendas can also be very informal. That is fine.
3. Adjust the Agenda Based on Other 1:1s
   - Some organizations require managers to meet quarterly with their team members around performance assessment and career development. If that is the case, there is less of a need to include these topics into your regular 1:1s—although it should still happen to support these broader efforts.
4. Focus on the Direct
   - Avoid having too many agenda topics of your own, thus taking time and focus away from the team member.
5. Connect Your Agenda with the Past
   - Be careful of a lack of coherence/continuity across meetings. When creating an agenda, consult the previous agenda. Repeat content where necessary to strengthen focus, but make sure to add new content to stimulate new paths and opportunities.
6. Take Post-Meeting Notes
   - As soon as the 1:1 meeting finishes, jot down ideas for the next 1:1 (e.g., items not covered due to time, an item to follow up on). These ideas will be most clear right after the meeting and will be the best way to prepare for the next 1:1 meeting. These notes will also help 1:1s build off each other and gain momentum.
7. Keep 1:1s Lightweight
   - There are lots of great questions that can be used in 1:1s in this book. But don't get crazy with asking a barrage of questions as it can prevent a good and deep conversation from occurring.
8. Be Adaptable
   - Space must be created for the direct to steer the conversation more organically in the meeting itself. In other words, have a plan, but be flexible. Don't be rigid. It's okay to go off script.

Don't worry about covering every item on the agenda; just hit the high priority items and know you can save remaining items for future conversations and 1:1s.

9. Adjust to Frequency
   - The need for structure in 1:1s is higher the more infrequent they are. Namely, if you are not getting much regular contact with your direct, when you do have 1:1 contact, you want to be sure to have broad and intentional coverage of key topics.
10. Lean into Directs' Needs
    - If your direct is focusing on a particular agenda item and they keep talking, let them as clearly this is something on their mind. You can cover your agenda items in a different mechanism if necessary.

Key Takeaways

- **Agendas Support Effectiveness.** Whether or not to have an agenda in 1:1s is a divisive question, but the data support their use. While setting up agendas (either before the meeting or at the start of the meeting itself) will take some time, they can improve the effectiveness and value of 1:1s.
- **Directs Must Contribute to the Agenda.** Agendas support 1:1 effectiveness and value, but only if the direct contributes to them. As a manager, do not create the agenda by yourself. Instead, have your direct draft up the agenda or create it together. Doing so will ensure alignment on what you will discuss in the meeting as well as increase the focus on direct's work and needs—the primary purpose of these meetings.
- **Two Models of Agenda Creation Are Most Recommended by Managers.** The listing approach has both you and your direct write down a list of topics to discuss. These items are then compared, and a final agenda is created. The core question approach, on the other hand, starts with a list of questions managers bring to their directs, which are broad enough to let the direct take control of the meeting content. Regardless of

which approach you take, make sure to start off and close the meetings strongly by building rapport and creating a psychologically safe space to engage fully.

- **Avoid the Status Update Trap.** You fall into this trap when 1:1s are focused on highly tactical, short-term topics—essentially asking your direct for a status update each meeting. You can avoid this trap by dedicating part of every 1:1 or all of some 1:1s to future-oriented topics, or by integrating these topics into the meeting agenda via a template.
- **Track Metrics (Sometimes).** Metrics can provide both you and your direct insight into how your direct is performing. However, you don't want to track these in every 1:1 because it can take away from their purpose and feel like micromanaging. Instead, the data suggest that metrics should be tracked in just some 1:1s if appropriate to the role and the metrics are indeed something the direct can control. Remember, it is key to go underneath the metrics: the "why" as it leads to conversation around achieving success, barriers to success, and support needed for success.

Section 1 Tools

Six tools are shared here to set the stage for your 1:1s:

1. Quiz to Determine Your Overall 1:1 Meeting Skills
2. Quiz to Determine Your 1:1 Meeting Cadences
3. Common Mistakes in 1:1 Questions
4. Special 1:1 Questions for Remote Employees
5. 1:1 Agenda Template
6. 1:1 Agenda Template with Add-Ons

Quiz to Determine Your Overall 1:1 Meeting Skills

This tool is designed to assess your 1:1 meeting skills. Reflect on each question and answer honestly. Periodically take this assessment to chart progress in 1:1 skill development.

Directions:

Reflect on all of your 1:1s conducted say, in the past 6 months to a year. For each question, indicate the percentage of time you have done the action/behavior. When answering, think about how your direct report(s) would respond, to keep yourself honest.

Quiz:

In your 1:1s, how often do you . . .	Percentage of Time Used (%)
1. Schedule 1:1s, in advance, on a reoccurring basis?	
2. Have some type of agenda for your 1:1s?	
3. Involve your direct(s) in the creation of the agenda?	
4. Review notes from the previous 1:1 before your next 1:1?	
5. Promptly reschedule cancelled 1:1s?	
6. Start 1:1s positively?	
7. Show up on time?	
8. Start with topics provided by your direct(s)?	

In your 1:1s, how often do you . . .	Percentage of Time Used (%)
9. Briefly revisit action items of the previous 1:1?	
10. Actively listen to your direct(s) during the meetings?	
11. Paraphrase things your direct(s) says?	
12. Talk less than your directs during the meeting?	
13. Ask powerful and meaningful questions?	
14. Adjust to what your direct(s) wants to talk about?	
15. Find yourself fully present during the meetings?	
16. Talk about nonwork topics?	
17. Check on the well-being of your direct(s)?	
18. Address roadblocks by providing resources/help?	
19. Take notes during the 1:1?	
20. Discuss topics other than status updates (e.g., long-term topics)?	
21. End on time?	
22. End with action items?	
23. Thank your direct(s) for their time and hard work?	
24. Summarize what was discussed?	
25. Share notes on the 1:1 once done?	
26. Contact your direct(s) outlining post 1:1 actions?	
27. Get feedback from your direct(s) on your 1:1s?	
28. Follow up on your promised action items?	
29. Follow up with your direct(s) on their action items?	

Scoring & Interpretation:

In the quiz, circle all values at or above 85% for each row. Then, count number of values you circled and write that number in the bottom row as your score.

If you circled . . .

- **26–29 (Excellent):** Great job! Keep up your good habits and try out some new skills/ideas based on learnings from the book.
- **20–25 (Opportunities exist):** You have a solid base of 1:1 skill, but you also have clear opportunity to excel further.
- **Less than 20 (Meaningful opportunities exist):** You will get a ton of guidance from the book to turn this score into a 29!

Quiz to Determine Your 1:1 Meeting Cadences

Complete this tool for each direct to identify the cadence that works best for that person. Circle the response that best fits the direct you are focusing on.

Category	Question
Remote vs. In-Person	**Is your direct:** 0) Mostly Onsite 1) 50% Onsite/50% Offsite 2) Mostly Offsite
Direct Preference	**Does your direct want to meet:** 0) Unsure/Doesn't Really Want to Meet 1) Sometimes 2) Often
Direct Experience	**For the role, is your direct:** 0) Experienced 1) Somewhat Experienced 2) Fairly Inexperienced
Direct Tenure	**How long has your direct been in the organization for:** 0) 5+ Years 1) 2–4 Years 2) Less than 1 Year
Manager Tenure	**How long have you managed your direct for:** 0) 2+ Years 1) 6 Months to 2 Years 2) Less than 6 Months
Team Size	**Is your team:** 0) Large (10+ directs) 1) Medium (5–9 directs) 2) Small (1–4 directs)
Weekly Staff Meetings	**Do you have weekly staff meetings:** 0) Yes 1) No

Category	Question
Use of Other Technologies	**You use asynchronous project management tools and applications (e.g., Google Docs) to monitor and address updates and challenges.** 0) Frequently 1) Sometimes 2) Infrequently
Total Score: ________	

Scoring & Interpretation:

Add up your total score on the quiz, then plot your score on the following thermometer graphic to find a suggested cadence for this direct. Be sure to work with your direct to see if this cadence fits, and reassess periodically. When in doubt, defer to the more frequent cadence.

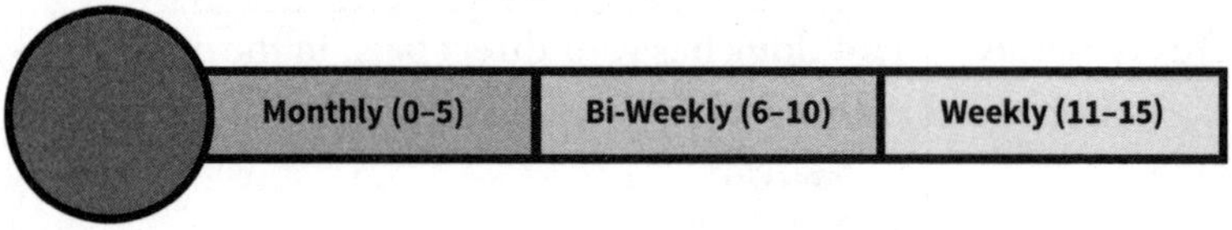

Common Mistakes in 1:1 Questions

Use this tool to acquaint yourself with the types of questions not to ask in a 1:1.

Common Question Mistakes	Examples	Used?
Getting too into the Weeds	Can you tell me about everything you've done this week in detail?	[ ]
Getting too Personal	I'm curious, do you go to church?	[ ]
Gossiping	Did you hear about what [employee] did last week?	[ ]
Ranting & Complaining	Our CEO is such a mess; do you like them?	[ ]
Focusing Only on Your Work	Can we start by talking about some support I need on my sales presentation?	[ ]
Extensively Discussing Other People on the Team	How are each of your peers doing on the job?	[ ]

Special 1:1 Questions for Remote Employees

The purpose of this tool is to provide you with 1:1 questions of particular relevance remote employees.

Questions for Remote Directs	Examples	Used?
Transition to Remote Work	• How is the transition to remote work going? • Is there anything you need to be successful in your new remote work environment?	[ ]
Work–Life Balance	• Are you able to set boundaries for work and life while working remotely?	[ ]
Benefits of Remote Work	• What's the best part(s) about working remotely?	[ ]
Challenges of Remote Work	• What's the most challenging part(s) about working remotely? • How can we address them?	[ ]
Extra Support Needed	• Is your remote work setup the best it could be? If not, what could help improve it? • Do you get the support you need? If not, what can we do to improve that support?	[ ]
Connection to the Team	• Do you feel connected to the team working remotely? • Are there any team member(s) you don't know as well due to working remotely that you want me to better connect you with?	[ ]
Inclusion in the Team	• Is there anything our team could do differently to make you feel more a part of the team as a remote employee?	[ ]

Questions for Remote Directs	Examples	Used?
Involvement in the Team	• Do you feel like you can voice your opinions/thoughts when working with the team as a remote employee?	[ ]
Career Development	• Do you have enough opportunities to develop your career as a remote employee? • Is there any area(s) of the team and/or organization that you would like to learn more about that you may not have access to as a remote employee?	[ ]

1:1 Agenda Template

A potential agenda template for your 1:1s is provided. You can certainly use whatever template/agenda structure you see fit, but this serves as a starting point you can work with. If you pursue this approach, the template can be used as either a physical printed document or virtual document.

Direct's Name:		
Date and Time:		
Key Goals & Projects	**Current Progress**	**Projected Results & Deadlines**
Write down major goals/projects listed by priority.	*Write down current progress on goals/projects and what support might be needed*	*Write down deadlines to note to keep your direct on track.*

Topic	**Notes**
Opening	*Write down wins, recognition, and highlights to start the 1:1 well.*
Review of Previous 1:1 Action Items	*Record discussion points from previous 1:1 action items & progress that need to be followed up on. Can be left blank if follow-up isn't needed.*
Today's Key 1:1 Priorities	*List you and your direct's highest priorities to cover for this meeting.*

Direct's Agenda Items	**Notes**
Your direct's agenda items listed by priority.	*Take notes during the 1:1 here.*
Manager's Agenda Items	**Notes**
Managers agenda items listed by priority (as time allows).	*Take notes during the 1:1 here.*
Long-Term Topics (Monthly)	**Notes**
Document longer-term topics to discuss such as career planning, development opportunities, and coaching.	*Take notes during the 1:1 here.*
Key Action Items & Next Steps	
<u>Manager</u> *A list of key action items you are responsible for*	<u>Direct</u> *A list of key action items your direct is responsible for*

1:1 Agenda Template with Add-Ons

The following content provides some additional options to add to your 1:1 template/agendas as desired/needed over time.

Topic	Notes
Wellness Scoring	*A rating of 1–10 for how your direct is feeling about their work life which is then discussed briefly at the start of the meeting. You can also attach a scoring option around other topics too (e.g., feeling like they are adding value).*
Manager Blindspot Updates	**Notes**
Direct shares anything they might want you to know about their work or life that you may not know about but may need to know to best support them.	*Take notes during the 1:1 here.*
Metric Tracker	**Notes**
A review of key metrics (e.g., performance) for directs used from time to time.	*Take notes during the 1:1 here.*
Feedback for Managers	**Notes**
A place for your direct to share feedback with you about anything, including how the 1:1s are going.	*Take notes during the 1:1 here.*
	Notes

Monitoring/ Aligning/ Supporting		
Key Goals & Projects	**Current Progress**	**Projected Results & Deadlines**
Write down major goals/projects listed by priority.	*Write down current progress on goals/ projects and what support might be needed*	*Write down deadlines to note to keep your direct on track.*

SECTION 2

CARRYING OUT 1:1S

In this section of the book I share a general model for conducting 1:1s so that both the personal and practical needs of directs are met. You will be walked through the steps for conducting effective 1:1s from start to finish. Although the leader plays a key facilitating role during 1:1s, the direct is not just a passive recipient. The key roles and responsibilities of directs are also shared to maximize positive value and impact of the experience.

1:1 are a tremendous opportunity to build rapport and relationships with your team through meaningful and genuine conversations. This, in turn, is critical to fostering trust. Trust is fundamental to team success. With trust, the team can reach new heights and push through the challenging and difficult times.

Executive, International Flavors

As we embrace the inevitability of modern work, the role of constructive 1:1 interaction as building blocks for an inclusive, high-performing organization is increasingly more significant.

Any executive that takes 1:1 meetings lightly is suboptimizing the ability to increase performance and effectiveness.

Executive, Marriott International

8

Is There a General Model for Conducting 1:1s?

In the world of Harry Potter, if you want to assure your success in anything you attempt you could make a good Felix Felicis (AKA Liquid Luck) potion. To create such a potion, you carefully follow a process involving ashwinder egg, quill bulb, murtlap tentacles, tincture of thyme, occamy eggshell, powdered common rue. You then wave your wand in particular ways, brewing for certain amounts of time, the potion is completed, and future success is all but assured. In the world of 1:1s, sadly, there is not a single formula or magical process that will invariably lead to success. There is, however, one thing we know for sure. Whatever process is done, you—as the manager—need to act like an orchestrator and a facilitator, and not a dominator (or a dementor, for that matter). In fact, the biggest predictor of 1:1 value I have found in my research is the direct report's active participation, as measured by the amount of time they talk during the meeting, relative to the manager. The ideal balance appears to be the direct speaking anywhere between 50% and 90% of the time. While the agenda will dictate some of this, the manager should actively avoid talking more than the direct report. This is not as easy as it sounds, given research showing that talking about ourselves fires up the same brain areas as sex and good food—we talk about ourselves because it feels good. But resist the temptation. Give this gift to the direct, and you, the manager, can focus on facilitating a great process and engaging deeply with what your direct shares.

Let me share what this could look like. Note, this chapter is just teeing up an approach to 1:1s. The goal here is to first expose you to an overview of the process so you can see the big picture. Then the other chapters in this section will unpack all of the elements and give you the details you'll need to be successful. My hope is that seeing the broad view will help contextualize the subsequent chapters.

An Integrated 1:1 Process

The 1:1 model described in this book integrates perspectives and approaches advocated for in the communication, coaching, facilitation, mentoring, meetings, and negotiation literatures. To understand the model, it is useful to acknowledge the ultimate goals of the model and what it is designed to accomplish. This is where I want to give special recognition to the excellent work of Dr. Tacy Byham.[1] Her work does such a great job of highlighting the two types of needs to be fulfilled in a successful 1:1 process. Namely, an excellent 1:1 process addresses directs' practical and personal needs. Practical needs are more tactical in nature. They can vary extensively, but ultimately, they are about advancing work, careers, projects, building alignment, and establishing priorities. Personal needs are about how a team member *feels* coming out of the 1:1—the need to feel trusted, respected, included, and the like. The figure that follows illustrates examples of these two sets of needs:

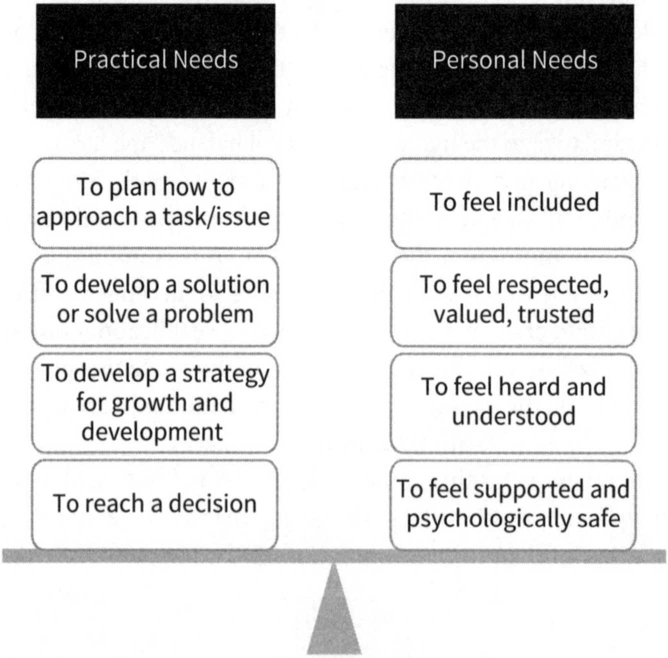

The ideal 1:1 process balances these two sets of needs. Meeting practical needs but failing to meet personal needs disturbs this balance and ultimately results in a loss. It is like getting a great product, but with horrible service. Similarly, meeting personal needs but failing on practical needs is also a loss—akin to getting great service but a bad product. You may ask, is filling one set of needs more important than the other? We can look to the leadership literature for a potential answer. Two sets of general leader behaviors have been extensively studied in the research: initiating structure (task-oriented) behaviors and consideration (relationship-oriented) behaviors.

Initiating structure behaviors are about communicating responsibilities, facilitating task and goal completion, clarifying roles and work, and the like. This not unlike behaviors associated with meeting the practical needs of directs. Conversely, consideration behaviors refers to the extent to which a leader expresses concern, demonstrates respect, and expresses support for their directs' welfare. This is all similar to behaviors associated with meeting the personal need of directs. Research has found that initiating structure behaviors are associated with leader job performance and group performance, while consideration behaviors are associated with satisfaction with the leader. In addition, both initiating structure, and even more so consideration, are related to directs' motivation as well as overall perceptions of leader effectiveness.[2] Thus, behaviors designed to fulfill personal and practical needs are both critical, with personal need fulfillment perhaps even a bit more so.

How to assure personal needs are met in 1:1s will be extensively discussed in the next chapter, but the key behaviors needed to do so are:

1. Listen and Respond with Empathy
2. Communicate Authentically and Transparently
3. Involve Directs Appropriately
4. Be Kind and Supportive
5. Demonstrate Appropriate Vulnerability

These behaviors all speak to the process and approach underlying the operational steps of 1:1s. Using the analogy mentioned earlier, they are about "the service" received rather than the product or result. Next, there are the operational steps. These steps are analogous to the frame of a house. They are the structure of the 1:1. These steps are discussed extensively in Chapter 10, but have the following key components:

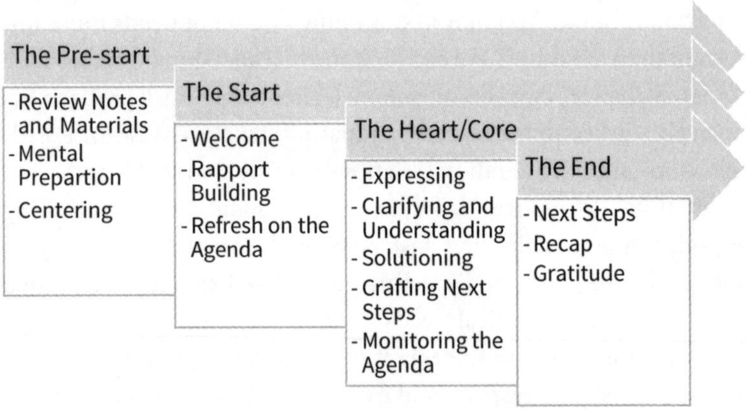

Note-Taking

A final element to the 1:1 model is note-taking by both parties. Notes capture key takeaways and actions, the essence of conversations, and the topics discussed in 1:1s. Notes capture developmental opportunities and performance concerns. Notes capture your private comments/observations about topics. Taking notes in your 1:1s makes you significantly less likely to forget or miss something of importance from the 1:1. Notes also allow you to notice and track changes (e.g., topics, concerns, and problems changing) over time. Taking notes can help you organize the actions each party has agreed to take. Additionally, a key part of preparation is reviewing past notes. Thus, without good notes, preparation is hampered. Finally, research shows that when you take notes, your brain better organizes the information you're hearing and encodes it more readily into your memory. With this all said, there is no need for voracious notetaking, as it can serve to be a distraction during the meeting and can keep you from being fully present. The goal is not to document *all* parts of the conversation, but to capture important points, actions, and highlights.

Although you certainly can take notes on a computer or use an app on your phone or computer to capture meeting content (e.g., Otter. AI), I'm personally partial to the old-school pen and paper option. My reasoning is twofold. First, this approach makes it clear you are paying attention and not multitasking. Second, if your 1:1 is in-person, there isn't a laptop/computer screen between you and your direct, which increases individual presence. As a related aside, if you prefer a digital copy, some parties choose to transcribe their written notes at the end of the meeting so all can be better archived, organized, and shared.

Putting this all together, the general 1:1 model that will be explored in the next chapters is as follows:

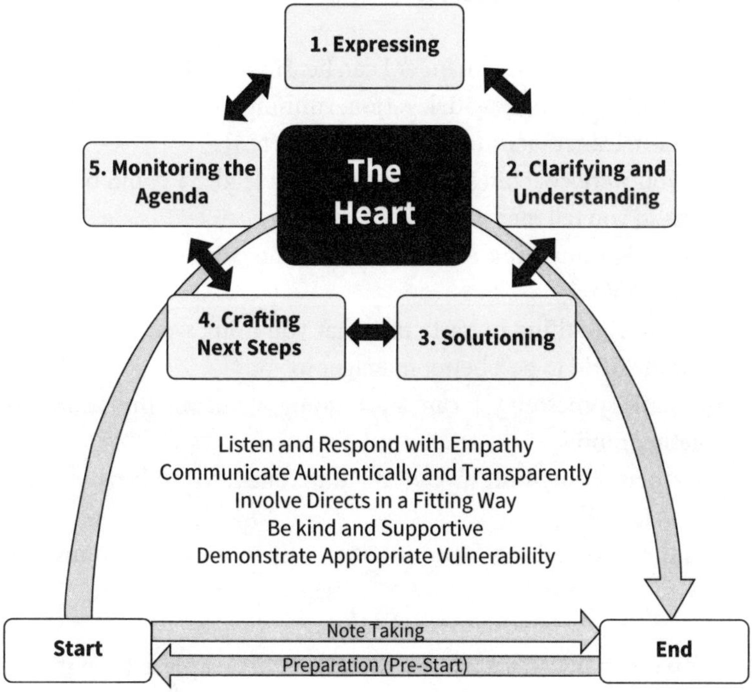

An Optional Process Step

Periodically and optionally, an additional step can be added to the 1:1 process, which would happen right before the end phase of the meeting: *manager seeking feedback*. This step has a very different feel to it, so it is worth calling out uniquely. It is a step in the 1:1 process that is specifically for the leader, which in many ways is counter to the overall goals of the 1:1. However, the direct can still ultimately benefit from it if you use the feedback to make positive changes.

In this step, you solicit feedback on your managerial behavior and actions from the team member. Specific inquiries are typically easier for the direct to address rather than broad questions such as, "How am I doing as your manager?" Let me reiterate some specific questions I shared in Chapter 6 and add some others that can help you with getting meaningful feedback:

- I want to be the best manger I can be. How can I improve on (insert different topics—delegation, running meetings, communication, team dynamics, prioritization, etc.)?
- If you were coaching me to be the best leader I could be, what would you tell me?
- What is something I should start doing, stop doing, and continue doing?
- Is there anything in particular that you think would be helpful for me to do to be a better manager to you?
- What's something I can start doing to bring the team together more?
- Is there something I can do differently to address <insert problem>?
- Is there something I can do differently in how I communicate with the team?

Remember, it isn't easy for directs to give upward feedback, even when prompted. Therefore, it's critical to reinforce and reward directs right away for giving their feedback. After you've prompted the feedback and digested what they've had to say, follow up with an expression of gratitude and appreciation for their transparency. If you want to keep getting feedback, you must reward it. You don't always have to respond to their feedback in the moment; rather, you can thank them for being candid and reflect afterwards.

Next, if applicable, show that you've listened and that you're making the necessary changes, even if it happens in small steps. Chapters 12 and 13 talk more about initiating your behavior change. However, this is if you agree with the feedback. This begs the question: What if you *disagree* with the feedback? It's still important to thank your team member for their bravery in sharing their thoughts. Let them know that you'll think about their comments, and then search for something reasonable in their comments that you can get on board with. After this, if needed, try scheduling a follow-up meeting to discuss points of disagreement and/or why you are not able to act on their all or some of their comments. One key in all of this is that you never, never, never want to punish the messenger. In fact, do just the opposite. Celebrate the messenger with a big thank you.

I want to add, if you suspect that your directs will not feel comfortable providing feedback (which makes a ton of sense given the power dynamic), try the feedforward technique discussed in Chapter 11. Feedforward, pioneered by Marshall Goldsmith, focuses on future behaviors rather than focusing on what went wrong in the past. Doing so makes it is easier for the direct to share remarks. Basically, it is an approach where you declare a developmental goal for yourself, like being a better delegator. Then, you ask your direct for their advice on how leaders in general can be great delegators. This way, feedforward is nonjudgmental, focused on the future, and dials the pressure down given that the conversation is not grounded in discussing actual problematic observations or behaviors.

Ultimately, seeking feedback demonstrates your commitment to becoming a better leader and improving on your growth areas. In turn, knowing that you're open to learning about your growth areas and areas of potential improvement makes it easier for others to give feedback and likely makes it easier for you to provide feedback in turn when relevant. Researchers studied 51,896 leaders and found that leaders who ask for feedback are perceived as stronger leaders than those who do not.[3] Although 1:1s are about your directs, this is a great example of how 1:1s can make you better as well.

Key Takeaways

- **Practical Versus Personal Needs.** Practical needs are tactical, focusing on how directs can successfully accomplish their work and advance their career. Personal needs are relational, focusing on how directs feel coming out of 1:1s (e.g., included, heard, valued, respected, supported, trusted). Both are needed for effective 1:1s. The key is to balance them within your meetings.
- **An Integrated Model.** While there isn't a secret formula for conducting effective 1:1s, there is a general model you can use. Four stages, which are discussed more in later chapters, embody this model: pre-start, start, the heart, and the end. The structure of the model—along with the questions to be asked that were previously discussed—help address directs' practical needs. Throughout each step, managers must also enact the five key relational behaviors mentioned (e.g., "Listen and Respond with Empathy") to meet directs' personal needs. When combined, this integrated model can support your 1:1 effectiveness.
- **Note-Taking is Helpful.** Taking notes during 1:1s creates accountability and documentation to increase the effectiveness of your 1:1s. Doing so helps you better organize what is discussed in 1:1s as well as increases the chances you don't miss anything. Notes can also allow you to follow up on action items or cover topics not discussed. When taken consistently, notes create momentum between 1:1s by allowing them to build off each other.

- **Ask for Feedback.** While this is an optional process step, asking for feedback from your directs periodically can further enhance 1:1 value. It also sends a strong message that you want to be the best manager you can be. If you decide to ask for feedback, always listen carefully, respond with gratitude, and explain what will be changed (or what won't be and why).

9

What Do I Do to Meet the Personal Needs of Others?

It was not that long ago that children would work long hours in factories. It was not that long ago that labor could legally occur in toxic and unsafe environments. It was not that long ago that you could fire someone for being pregnant or having a disability. In fact, just over 100 years ago, the thought of having a Human Resources department in your company was met with great skepticism. Now, it is generally recognized that elevating the human condition at work is not just the right thing to do, but a business imperative—we know that employee feelings about their job and employer affect their customer service, productivity, helping of others, safety in the workplace, teamwork, innovation, and retention. It even relates to the organization's bottom line financial results. For example, companies with employees reporting higher levels of psychological safety (the belief you can speak up and engage with the job without fear of humiliation or punishment) perform better financially than companies with employees reporting lower levels of psychological safety.[1] Although employees' feelings, emotions, and attitudes about the job and organization are influenced by many different factors, 1:1s play a pivotal role given their focus on addressing the direct's practical needs. However, of key relevance in this chapter, 1:1s also address the personal needs (e.g., feeling respected and included) of the team member.

To figure out how to best address personal needs, I first surveyed directs and managers about the topic. Then, I consulted the published research. For instance, one study found that feeling listened to by your leader was associated with greater feelings of psychological safety.[2] Integrating my data with this research, five interrelated categories of behaviors emerged as key to promoting personal needs satisfaction:

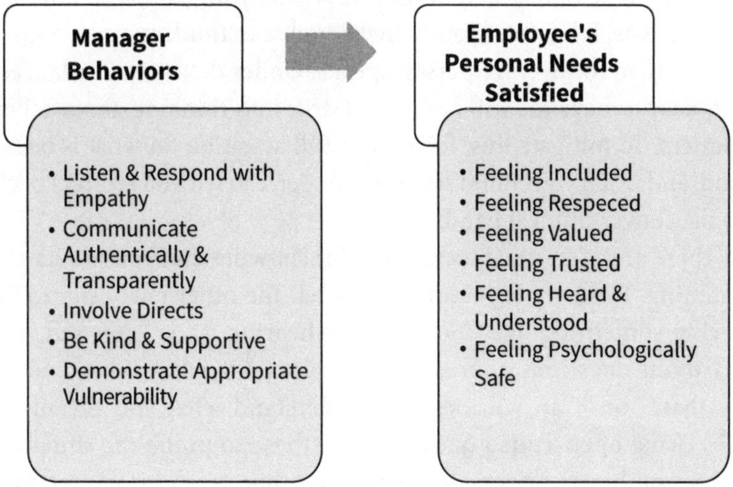

Listen and Respond with Empathy

Two quotes from two very different people help illustrate the essence of this behavioral category:

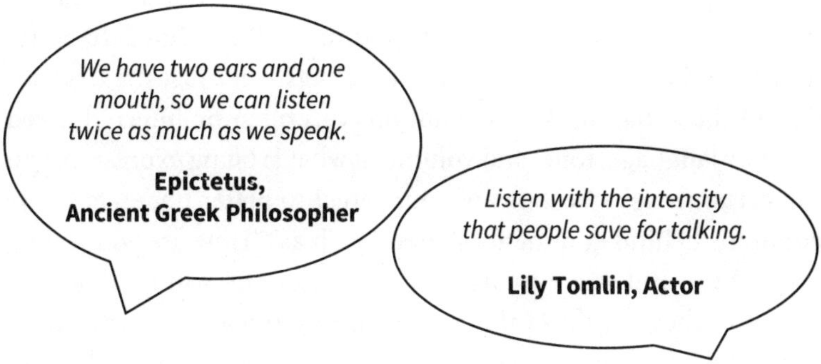

When listening is coupled with empathy, conversations are significantly enhanced and serve to help the other person feel heard, understood, and truly seen. I will start with the listening piece. Listen to absorb what your direct is saying rather than listening to respond. To listen effectively we need to remove distractions. There is, however, one type of distraction that we typically forget about: internal distractions. It has been found that people can think at much higher speeds than the average person speaks. Under those circumstances, it is easy to have the listener's mind drift into thinking about other matters. To mitigate this, focus your full attention on what is being said, and when your mind starts to wonder, catch it and redirect back to the conversation at hand.

There are a few great techniques for showing that you're actively listening. First, try repeating back what the other party shares by saying something like, "So what I'm hearing is. . . ." Second, ask clarifying questions such as, "When you said X, what did you mean by that?" or "Can you help me understand what you meant by Y?" Using open-ended questions like these to probe the situation helps you better understand what the other person is expressing. Furthermore, it is likely that the answers shared will prompt additional questions, which is what active engagement as a listener is all about. The goal in using this technique is to build an understanding of their situation, and once clarity occurs, the questions can stop.

The empathy part of the equation can be a bit more challenging. With empathy, you are attempting to see things from the perspective of the other person. You are "putting on their shoes" to better understand and connect with their feelings—not just the description of the situation. While emotions can often be inferred based on body language, tone, and volume of what is being expressed, you can certainly ask questions of your direct to better understand the emotions behind comments shared (such as, "How are you feeling about X?"). But more than likely, the emotions will be quite apparent as they speak. At that point, you should acknowledge their feelings with comments such as "that sounds really trying," "I am so sorry to hear this," "that must be very difficult," and "I can see why that would be frustrating." You can also demonstrate empathy by sympathetically sharing how you feel about what you just heard, such as with, "oh wow, it makes me sad to hear this." The key to all the above is being genuine and being and open-minded to other's "truths" in a nonjudgmental way. Otherwise, the team member could feel patronized.

After achieving a better understanding and connection to the words of your direct, I encourage you to express gratitude to the person for sharing their feelings ("Thank you for sharing, that means a lot to me."). You can also offer support—which we will talk more about later—with statements such as, "I want to be here for you, what can I do?" Remember that empathy isn't synonymous with agreement, it is about demonstrating your full understanding of a situation and the experience of your team member.

Communicate Authentically and Transparently

1:1s are all about communication. Communicating well is an essential piece to meeting the personal needs of the direct. At the core of this big category of behaviors is effectively providing both positive and constructive feedback to your team members. Namely, team members should understand your expectations and, on an ongoing basis, know about where they are meeting the mark and where there is need for improvement. This sound easy, but clearly in practice, it is not. For example, in a global study consisting of nearly 900 participants, 72% of employees indicated that their manager did not provide critical feedback despite them wanting it.[3] This is consistent with the extant research on how managers avoid or are reluctant to give constructive feedback to their employees.[4]

Curious about how all of these findings apply to people by generation? Research suggests that individuals from every generational group sampled (Baby Boomers, Gen X, and Millennials) were open to positive feedback as well as constructive feedback (even more so than positive). In general, counter to conventional stereotypes, the older respondents were most desirous of feedback—both positive and constructive.[5]

Previous research suggests that reticence to give constructive feedback is because managers are concerned about the negative interpersonal consequences it might have.[6] Moreover, managers do not feel motivated to put in the effort that delivering constructive feedback requires—especially with the potential to have these negative effects.[7] However, it seems that the most common reason feedback is not given is that leaders underestimate the value that giving feedback can have for their directs.[8] The above three reasons create a cycle of not giving feedback—a problem that we and our 1:1s can rectify.

Prior to giving feedback, make sure that your behavior and actions on the job are consistent with the behavior you are asking others to engage in. To do otherwise sends a confusing message to the direct: "Do as I say, not as I do." At the same time, feedback tends to be the most well-received when it's solicited by the recipient. In the absence of this, you can still ask your direct if they would like feedback on X or if you can share some feedback around Y that you have observed. They will invariability say "yes," but this simple question does help pave the wave for a bit more receptivity, allays blindsiding, and offers a nice segway into the conversation.

Feedback should be appropriate, specific, timely, behavioral, and descriptive rather than broad, and evaluative (e.g., "You are just not doing a good job"). By focusing on more specific behaviors of concern, the direct is better able to see what they need to do to correct. Or, in the case of praise, the specificity serves to encourage continuing of certain behaviors. It is important that the feedback you share addresses behaviors that are under the direct's control. Getting feedback on behaviors one does not control can be quite demotivating (e.g., telling someone they need to process their orders more quickly if the operational system to process orders is broken). Also, choose what you give feedback on wisely. Don't focus on behaviors that may be just stylistic differences, too nit-picky, or not all that important. As Winston Churchill once said, "perfection is the enemy of progress."

Finally, feedback can be about behaviors to start, to continue, or to stop. Let me say a bit more about stop behaviors, as they may be less clear. I really like the ten stop behaviors Marshall Goldsmith offers as potential candidates to address:[9]

1. **Winning Too Much**: The need to win at all costs and in all situations.
2. **Adding Too Much Value**: The overwhelming desire to add our two cents to every discussion.
3. **Making Destructive Comments**: Needless sarcasm and cutting remarks.
4. **Speaking When Angry**: Using their emotional volatility to get attention and lead others.
5. **Negativity, or "Let me explain why that won't work"**: The need to share our negative thoughts even when we weren't asked.
6. **Withholding Information**: The refusal to share information to maintain an advantage over others.
7. **Failing to Give Proper Recognition**: The inability to give praise and reward.
8. **Claiming Credit that We Don't Deserve**: Overestimating contributions to any success.
9. **Refusing to Express Regret**: The inability to take responsibility for our actions, admit we're wrong, or recognize how our actions affect others.
10. **Passing the Buck**: The need to blame everyone but ourselves.

Feedback given should be balanced between constructive positive and constructive negative feedback. We tend to more readily see when people make mistakes and do things wrong than when they do things right. We must catch and reinforce people doing the right things. By sharing a more balanced picture in your feedback—that is genuine of course—feels fairer to the direct and is better received. John Wooden, the great UCLA basketball coach, was a big advocate of balanced feedback with his players. It was reported that in a typical practice session, he would give his player a ratio of three positive messages to every one improvement message. The positive feedback not only reinforced what he wanted to see more of, but it made it easier for people to accept the negative feedback. I can't say whether that is a magic ratio per se, but the spirit of this approach seems quite compelling. I do want to note that one study done by Glassdoor demonstrates the value of praise. They found that 53% of respondents reported that if they received more appreciation from their manger, they would likely stay with their employer longer.[10]

Regardless of whether the feedback is positive or negative, keep the focus on the behaviors in question and *not* the person. State the behavior that you want to provide feedback around, describe how you feel about it (good or bad), and finish with your suggestions going forward. Here is what this could sound like:

"I noticed the other day that customer X did not receive the follow-up materials they had asked for. I am concerned about that, as we don't want to lose them as a client. What is your take on the situation, and can you help me understand what may have happened?"

After they respond, this can be followed with your suggestions and ideas going forward. Contrast this behavior-focused feedback approach with a more person-focused feedback approach:

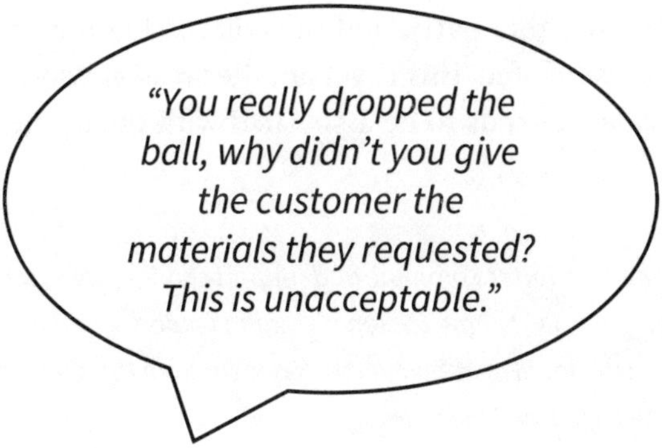
"You really dropped the ball, why didn't you give the customer the materials they requested? This is unacceptable."

It is easy to see how the behavior-focused approach allows for a more meaningful conversation with less defensiveness in which growth can more readily occur. You are still holding the person accountable, but it does not feel as judgmental, which is key. Relatedly, use "I" statements when delivering feedback. This communicates that your feedback is your opinion and acknowledges its inherent subjectivity. It represents *your* truth. As a result, it allows for more conversation about what happened and what to do rather than your feedback being the whole or only story.

Consider the cognitive load that your feedback will place on the receiver. Be realistic about what the direct can handle, and don't overwhelm them with a long list of improvement suggestions. Doing so can serve to paralyze and demotivate the recipient. Asking your direct to focus on one or two changes is probably enough, especially if they are key behaviors, as other behaviors will invariability be affected by positive changes. A narrower to-do list typically translates to more progress and success by the direct. By building momentum on a couple of key behaviors, and reinforcing it readily, it also paves the way for continued success as the direct will feel a greater sense of confidence in their ability to make changes.

Finally, immediate feedback is more impactful than delayed feedback. Reinforce or provide constructive feedback for the behavior soon after it happens. A long delay leads to foggy details which can derail the feedback effort. For example, discussing a problematic customer interaction you noticed 3 weeks prior will not be fully remembered by either party, and thus discussing it at present will likely not be as helpful. This is yet another reason why a more frequent 1:1 cadence tends to be associated with the greatest positive outcomes.

If after extensive efforts to promote and support change, the team member is still failing, it is likely time to stop providing feedback and instead consider exiting the team member. Removing them from the situation can be good for them, you, and the team.

In addition to providing feedback in an excellent manner, authentic and transparent communication in 1:1s has some other pieces I want to briefly mention:

1. Good leaders provide clear direction, and they share information readily and honestly.
2. Good leaders ask their people if they need information, and then seek to provide it.
3. Good leaders explain the reasons underlying decisions that impact their people.
4. Good leaders encourage their people to ask questions, and if they don't know the answer, they go the extra yard and seek it out.
5. Good leaders seek out communication gaps or ambiguities and actively work to fill them.

Finally, a good leader avoids spreading gossip and speaking ill of others. Besides just being inappropriate, by speaking ill of others, people will assume you will also speak poorly of them behind their backs. Relatedly, be careful of asking directs to keep secrets. In general, it's a good rule of thumb to not share information with a particular team member if you wouldn't share it with the entire team. Asking someone to keep a secret can put them in an uncomfortable position with their colleagues and can be experienced as a bit of a burden. It also reduces the sense of transparency and authenticity you are trying to cultivate within your team. With this all said, there are times when confidential communication is needed, but when this is the case, do it judiciously and only when truly necessary.

Involve Directs

Directs typically want a say in how they execute their work tasks, to be involved in the decision-making that concerns them, to share ideas about problems being confronted, and to have input around changes they have to implement. After all, they are living the job each hour and each day while at work. Their boots are on the ground. Involvement can be done readily in 1:1s by asking individuals for their opinions about an issue. For example you can ask, "What are your initial thoughts about addressing X?" There are four benefits to this approach. First, they've probably already thought of some solutions to the problem. Second, it communicates that you value their input and opinions, which makes them feel respected and valued. Third, it gives you insight into how your people think and solve problems. And fourth, we tend to be much more engaged with and committed to ideas we create or co-create. It is important to note that there are some natural limits to employee involvement. Not all decisions can and should include a team member's voice or input. Some broad, big, and multi-faceted decisions are just what they are. They roll down from above and all must align around them.

I often get asked, "Can a manager share their thoughts in the 1:1 around an issue or topic?" Of course. Share your opinions, insights, and ideas. However, do so after seeking others' input first. Relatedly, don't assume you know the best way to approach an issue. The way you handled it in the past might not be appropriate now. Your thoughts should not be framed as the "right" answer—just another perspective to consider and discuss unless of course there is just a single answer.

Be Kind and Supportive

Kindness is behavior marked by acts of generosity, consideration, and rendering assistance or concern for others, without expecting praise or reward in return. I don't want to lecture the reader on how to be kind. After all, our caretakers have been telling us about kindness since we were very young. In the case of 1:1s, one key to kindness is offering continuing support. Being in someone's corner and investing in them is an ultimate act of kindness. I do want to share two little caveats. First, help the person grow and develop by themselves, with your support, but be careful of fostering dependence. Second, enacting kindness does not mean you can't hold people accountable. Accountability and kindness are not mutually exclusive in any way. Sometimes, holding people accountable is an act of kindness in of itself. Overall, being kind is essential to addressing personal needs and building a robust relationship. It also allows your messages of accountability and/or critical feedback to be more readily heard, as you intend them as kindness can break down walls of defensiveness and close-mindedness. It is also noteworthy that kindness begets kindness. There is a contagious quality to it.[11]

Research has shown that being kind and helping others can even be good for your health. For example, being kind and helping others appears to mitigate the negative effects of stress you might be experiencing,[12] and in a more extreme example those senior citizens that engaged in volunteerism (a key kindness behavior) had a lower likelihood of dying early[13] and less likelihood of having hypertension.[14]

Demonstrate Appropriate Vulnerability

As the person in a position of power, you set the norm for your meetings to be a safe place to talk about fears, worries, challenges, and goals. So lead by example and be willing to be vulnerable and personal. Where appropriate, share your feelings to some extent—positive or negative—to show that you trust people and to encourage them to trust you. Appropriate vulnerability from the leader helps the direct feel safer and sets the stage for building a meaningful relationship. It also implicitly creates permission for the direct to follow suit and be vulnerable as well. Overall, let your meetings be humanizing. Relatedly, vulnerability necessitates a willingness to admit your mistakes to yourself and to your team; turn them into teachable moments to demonstrate that mistakes are not something to hide or blame on others. You can also use this opportunity to apologize to a team member for something you might have done or said.

Another part of appropriate vulnerability is asking for help from others. No one can have all the answers or know how to do everything. An appropriately vulnerable leader will ask team members for help from time to time (e.g., asking a team member to explain something, show you how to perform a task, or lend a helping hand). Asking others for help can also build the relationship. This notion has been termed the Franklin Effect, as Ben Franklin was known to do this with his rivals.[15] Furthermore, asking for help may increase the chances of your direct asking for your help when needed. And, again, doing so makes the relationship become deeper.

I must emphasize the word *appropriate* here, as you should be vulnerable, but not over the top. That is, be vulnerable, but don't overshare so much that it puts the focus of the 1:1 squarely on you and serves to make others uncomfortable. The goal is to share just enough so that the other party feels comfortable sharing as well. Find the right balance.

Taken together, these five behavioral categories work to meet personal needs in a doable and reasonable way. They do not require extraordinary effort. They can be achieved readily with attention and thoughtfulness. The outcomes will likely be your directs feeling included, respected, valued, trusted, heard, understood, supported, and psychologically safe. This is a huge win for the 1:1 and the relationship more broadly, and is at the heart of effective 1:1s. I also can't stress enough that these behaviors to satisfy personal needs, while certainly relevant to leaders and their directs, can be applied to any relationship building effort—be it with peers, family, friends, and/or customers.

Key Takeaways

- **Satisfying Personal Needs Is Critical.** While 1:1s are meant to address directs' practical needs, they must also be conducted in a way that meets directs' personal needs. Doing so ensures that directs feel included, respected, valued, heard, understood, and supported. Satisfying personal needs also builds a climate of psychological safety which can serve to elevate the 1:1 and enhance value.
- **Five Key Behaviors Are Needed to Meet Personal Needs.** There are five key behaviors needed to address direct's personal needs: 1) Listen and Respond with Empathy, 2) Communicate Authentically and Transparently, 3) Involve Directs, 4) Be Kind and Supportive, and 5) Demonstrate Appropriate Vulnerability. Each behavior is needed to support both 1:1 effectiveness and your relationship with your direct.

10

How Do I Start and End 1:1s—And the Middle Stuff Too?

In the last chapter we talked about the critical behaviors needed to address personal needs of the direct in 1:1s. In this chapter, we review the four logistical steps of 1:1s: Pre-Start, Start, The Heart, and End. Here is a refresher of the overall 1:1 model shared in Chapter 8 for context:

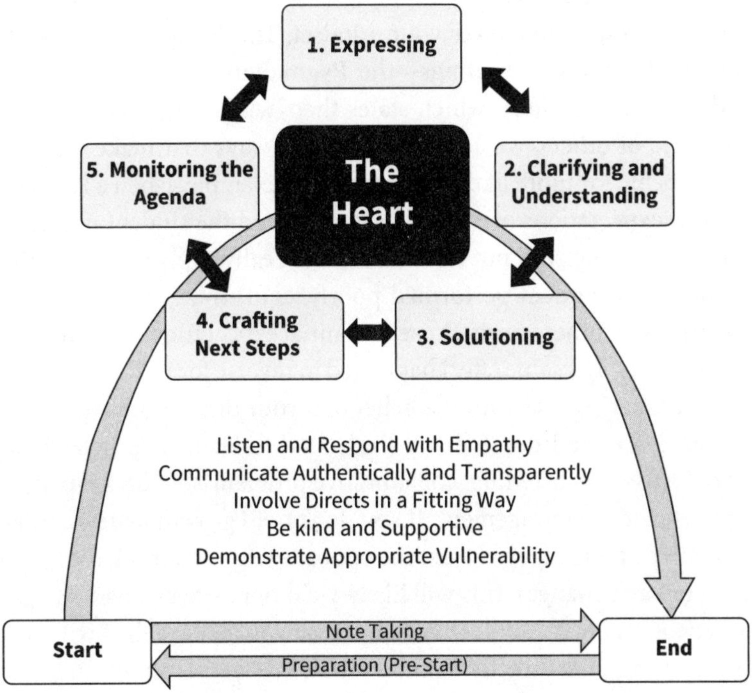

The 1:1 process above is not a magic formula. You can adjust and tweak the process so it works for you. Understand your team

members' styles and preferences so you can adjust as needed. Overall, flex your approach to meet people where they are.

Pre-Start and Start

As Benjamin Franklin so eloquently said, "By failing to prepare you are preparing to fail." Before you walk into that room, get on video, or take that walk, preparation is needed. Start with reviewing notes from the last 1:1 you had with your direct. What was discussed, what threads should continue to this next 1:1, and are there any items that should be followed up on? It is important to remember and reinforce the connective tissues between 1:1s to continue momentum and amplify positive outcomes.

Preparation also involves your mindset. This brings me to one of my favorite research findings—the Pygmalion effect, also known as the Rosenthal effect, which states that "when we expect certain behaviors of others, we are likely to act in ways that make the expected behavior more likely to occur."[1] For example, when a teacher had low expectations of a student, they treated the student in a certain manner (e.g., did not take the time to really explain things). By doing so, the student performed poorly, confirming the initial expectations. In other words, those low initial expectations became the actual reality. The same effect happened in reverse for positive expectations. Entering 1:1s with the belief that your direct wants to grow, change, learn, and develop will likely lead to leadership behaviors more focused on listening, collaborative problem-solving, empathy, support, and encouragement. If you don't hold growth beliefs about your direct, and in fact feel just the opposite (e.g., you think they just won't or can't change), this will likely yield opposite behaviors (e.g., not encouraging or supportive)—because you assume they will not help anyway. This directly counters what 1:1s are all about. In both cases, a self-fulfilling prophecy is likely to occur—your behaviors will likely lead to outcomes aligned with your initial expectations. Remember, if someone is truly a bad employee, document and address the problem over time and if necessary through exit. But most of the time, this is not the case. Therefore, when having 1:1s, positive expectations are needed to realize the full potential of the meetings and of your directs.

Let's move to the actual start of the 1:1. Begin with a quick discussion of nonwork-related topics, wins, and/or appreciation to build momentum and foster feelings of psychological safety. Take an interest in your direct as a person. Hopefully the agenda has been finalized in advance, but if not, that is okay. Simply finalize it at the start. The key is ensuring that everyone understands the meeting's desired outcomes and how you will get there. If the agenda was made in advance, always ask if there are any changes to be made before moving on. This is also a good time to ask, "what are the absolute musts we need to cover/get to before we end our time together?" so that you can prioritize time most appropriately. Finally, as I noted earlier, I like some quick reference to a past 1:1 (e.g., a quick check in on a problem or issue broached last 1:1 perhaps) as a way of showing the direct that these 1:1s matter to you and you are fully dialed into them. As part of starting, periodically emphasize certain norms you want to see enacted in the 1:1 such as candor, involvement, open-mindedness, and a commitment to transparency to set the stage for rich and sincere conversation.

The Heart

While the Pre-Start and Start are important to set the meeting up for success, The Heart is where the action happens. Each agenda item will be covered in this part of the 1:1, one at a time (most likely). There are five main interconnected phases to this free-flowing part of the model as you see in the figure. Depending on the agenda item in question, certain phases of the model may get more attention, and some could be skipped in their entirety. For example, if there is an information-only item, you will focus on just the expressing and clarifying/understanding phases of this process. Notice that all phases of the model are connected via double arrows, as the communication flow may be highly dynamic. Jumping around between phases is common and expected. For example, when in the solutioning phase, you may wind up going back to the clarifying/understanding phase to better understand the issue needing to be solved. Let's unpack each of these five phases to better understand the role they play in 1:1s. I also encourage you to review the Preparation Checklist for 1:1 Facilitation tool found at the end of this book section It is a quick primer you can glance at prior to the start of a 1:1 meeting.

Expressing Phase

The expressing phase is about getting topics and issues on the table regardless of whether you start with an agenda core question or if your direct starts with content from their list. Invite the direct in with encouraging words to get them talking. While it may be tempting to jump into topics related to your needs, don't. Focus on priority one first, namely your direct's content and needs. Be an appreciative recipient of what you hear. As part of this all, use welcoming body language to promote connection and suggest interest. Avoid positions that can convey being closed off and defensive (e.g., crossed arms). Whether in-person or virtual, use appropriate eye contact to help make your direct feels seen and heard.

Clarifying and Understanding Phase

This phase is about engaging with the content shared by the direct and working to fully understand what was said, including getting to the root cause(s) of issues. Active listening and asking powerful questions to explore points of view are key here, such as "tell me more about . . .", "what is your analysis of why this is happening", or "is there any history with similar situation that could be helpful to consider". See Chapter 9 for more discussion of techniques for listening, probing, and exploring.

Depending on the nature of the agenda item presented, you may next move to the solutioning phase after thoroughly understanding what was broached. Or perhaps the direct just wants to vent and for you to listen, and thus you can just sail back to the expressing phase to tee up the next agenda item. Or, perhaps solutioning started to naturally during the clarifying and understanding phase itself, through excellent question asking and careful listening. To simply illustrate, imagine an orange sitting on a table. George says, "I want the orange." Liana then says, "I want the orange." Clearly the two positions are incompatible with one another given there is only one orange. Thus, the solution that often would emerge through negotiation is either to cut the orange in half and share (a compromising solution), or only one party gets the orange and the other does not (a win–lose solution). However, there is an alternative: asking why the person holds the position they do—in this case, why they want the orange. Doing so helps figure out motives behind the desire. By asking why, a synergistic solution might just be found. Let me demonstrate this with the orange example, inserting "why" questions.

Liana: "I want the orange."
George: "Liana, why do you want the orange?"
Liana: "I am hungry and thirsty, and the orange will give me what I need."
George: "I want the orange."
Liana: "George, why do you want the orange?"
George: "I am making scones and need the orange rind."

Now that motives are clear, in this case a win–win solution can readily be found. Liana can get the inside of the orange, and George can take the rind. Both people are happy. While this is a silly example, asking "why" and probing what is shared changes the conversation and can allow you to readily find solutions you may not have discovered otherwise. Bottom line, by digging deeply into the clarifying and understanding phase, resolutions can start to emerge, propelling us into the solutioning phase.

Solutioning Phase

Solutioning will likely look different depending on the agenda item. This phase could include:

- Giving feedback and charting an improvement path forward
- Providing general counsel, support, suggestions, and advice
- Working through a specific problem, obstacle, or challenge and developing a plan
- Identifying available support and resources for your direct

The first part of solutioning is typically asking what ideas the direct has, given their closeness to the problem and the importance of them buying into any solution. Open-ended questions could include:

- "From your past experiences, do you have any thoughts on how to proceed?"
- "What is your gut telling you for how to address this issue and why?"
- "What two or three approaches might work, and what might be the pluses/minuses of each approach?"

Keep promoting idea generation; there is no need to accept the first option and you absolutely can and should constructively challenge ideas. Here is a key point, however, which I will bold, as it is common problem for leaders: **If the direct's solution does not fully align with yours, but it is still viable, go with <u>their</u> idea—even if you think yours is a bit better.** If you think there is a large gap in quality between your idea and theirs, and the consequences of a wrong solution are high, then it is reasonable to push back. "A large gap" with consequences is the meaningful phrase. If there isn't a big gap between your idea and theirs, the direct-generated solution is the better call, as the team member created it. Accepting their idea conveys that you trust them and their judgement, and promotes more commitment from the direct to take action and persevere in the face of obstacles. I do want to say, even in cases where you think there is a big gap between ideas in terms of quality, but there are *no meaningful negative* consequences associated with the direct's ideas if wrong, it likely is best to go with what the direct shared. If their solution does not work out down the road, you can certainly debrief together and try something different. But if it does work, it's a win–win for both of you. Overall, pick your battles and be reasonable. The direct should not have to match your solution every time, especially as you likely don't know for fact that your solution is the only path forward. Again, as mentioned in a previous chapter, I don't want you to think that you can't share your point of view in a 1:1. You certainly can and should. There are absolutely moments in 1:1s when you do need to contribute your point of view and/or share honest and specific feedback. But pick those times thoughtfully so they don't serve to demotivate and promote feeling of impotence in your directs.

The above steps may feel quite linear in nature—the direct goes first, the manager next, repeat. But, given that there is active questioning and exploring throughout the solutioning phase, the process should feel engaging, dynamic, and interactive. But what if neither the manager nor the direct has meaningful ideas to begin with? Brainstorm together and engage in collaborative problem solving. Work together to truly understand whatever issue is at hand, pooling information, identifying root causes, and creating a solution both parties feel good about. If you can't come up with a solution in that exact moment, that's fine, you can both sit with and reflect on it. Then, just circle back together—either offline or at the next 1:1—to discuss what you've thought about. It is also possible that the inability to find a meaningful solution could lead you back to the clarifying and understanding phase. This happens and is totally fine.

Get comfortable with silence as a manager. It can be tempting to want to fill the silence if and when it happens, but keep in mind that silence is often an indication of contemplation rather than awkwardness or a lack of engagement. You can even encourage moments of silence by telling your directs to pause whenever they need to so they can think through their ideas. This does not have to be a rushed process.

Crafting Next Steps Phase

Nail down what was agreed upon in solutioning. Great ideas are truly great only when someone acts on them, so get clarity on the final plan and next steps. As part of this conversation, ask directs what resources or support they need from you, and what steps they should take to get them if not from you. If the direct is not highly forthcoming about what is needed, you can also make suggestions of help you could provide (a resource, an introduction to a key person, getting involved in a conversation, etc.) and then ask the direct what they think. Be careful, though. If you agree to support someone, help the person as needed, but remember that they are ultimately responsible for completing the task.

When creating action items for you and your direct, I am a big fan of using the same approach that research on goal-setting advocates for. Action steps should be specific, measurable, achievable, realistic/relevant, and time-bound (the S.M.A.R.T. approach). Action items can range from large complex tasks to simple ones such as "make a list of goals for your team." It also might be the case that, given the particular agenda item in question, no action items are appropriate—a discussion may be sufficient.

Monitoring the Agenda

Work through the established agenda, but also be flexible to allow the conversation to move about organically. Focus on items that are most critical for your direct—which should be earlier in the agenda—to ensure the value of 1:1s. Ultimately, as the manager, you are responsible for managing meeting time, but you can still be flexible. Periodically check in with your direct during the 1:1 to be sure they are on target to get their needs met. While agendas are useful, do not let them cause you to superficially address important issues such that you rush through these items to be able to address the whole agenda. Focus on the important topics first. Remember, anything on that agenda that is not covered can be discussed at the next 1:1, or offline.

I want to stress again, all of these phases in the heart of the 1:1 are not necessarily completed in a linear order. They can be, but you may find that the conversation jumps around a lot to the various phases. It is totally fine either way. Finally, there are times when negative emotions can emerge during the course of the conversation. This happens. It just needs to be dealt with constructively. At the end of this book section you will find a tool for helping do this well. It is called: True/False Quiz on Skills for Dealing with Negative Emotions in 1:1s.

The End

Frist rule, end the 1:1 on time. Running over inadvertently communicates a lack of respect for others' time. It's okay to end a bit early if you've accomplished the goals of the meeting (if it is always ending early, however, that could be a signal that you are not effectively running the 1:1 and/or maximizing the time together). But, at the core of this phase of the 1:1 process is the need for a meaningful conclusion. And the conclusion should ideally lean positive (or at least not negative).

A classic study by Nobel Prize winner Daniel Kahneman and colleagues demonstrated the importance of the end of experience in affecting your future behavior.[2] The researchers assigned participants to two conditions in their experiment. In the first condition, participants submerged their hand in very cold water (14°C, 57°F) for 60 seconds. This is not as easy as it sounds. It is very uncomfortable. The second condition was identical, except 30 additional seconds were added where the participant kept their hand in slightly warmer water (15°C, 59°F). The temperature increase was not large, and it was still cold, but it was more comfortable, relatively speaking, than the first 60 seconds. They then asked participants in each condition if they would be willing to repeat the conditions. Those in the second condition were indeed more willing, despite being in uncomfortably cold water for longer. The difference: those in the second condition ended on a more positive note. This is an important finding which can easily be applied to 1:1s.

An excellent 1:1 conclusion has several pieces to it. Be sure takeaways, commitments, timelines, and action steps are clear for both parties, including how you will support next steps. If there are any last-minute thoughts or changes needed, they are totally fine for either party to broach here. To promote accountability and progress between meetings, jot down and later distribute quick notes capturing this content. The following quote from Andy Grove, former CEO and cofounder of Intel, sums this up well: "Equally important is what 'writing it down' symbolizes . . . the act implies a commitment, like a handshake, that something will be done."

Finally, end the 1:1 by thanking directs for their hard work. Praise them for the good efforts and/or results they have achieved. Even if you're having a tough conversation, or dealing with some constructive feedback, try to end on an affirming note. Whether that's with a statement like, "I know this is hard. We'll tackle it together," "This kind of feedback isn't always easy to receive; I want you to know I can see how much effort you are putting into this and I'm impressed by your openness to feedback. I'm glad you're part of the team," or some other encouragement or effort to increase the confidence of the direct. Ending on a positive will allow you to both leave the meeting feeling motivated and optimistic rather than stressed and drained.

Illustrations

Some quotes taken from interviews with team members/leaders when asked about excellent 1:1 experiences help bring the 1:1 process to life. In this first quote on what drives 1:1 effectiveness, balance is a clear theme:

> *"1) Opened on a personal note to check on my wellbeing and have a more personal interaction, 2) had right balance of time for me to communicate/discuss my items and for him to do the same, 3) allowed for coaching to take place. He also makes sure there is time for more sensitive topics and is a very good listener. It is clear that he is present and interacting with me authentically."*

This next quote does a nice job describing a potential 1:1 structure, as well as the role of the manager in prompting the direct to think deeply:

> *"We have a set structure-we talk about my core responsibilities, my progress on projects and my progress on my evolution in my development. We have a simple scorecard that keeps everything visible and conscious for all of us. My manager gives short clear feedback and tons of assignments for self-reflection -asking me to check things out for myself and to notice and learn about my own way through the world".*

The last quote captures the importance of different types of 1:1s and the importance of asking questions:

"There are two types of 1:1 meetings. Some are tactical and focused on goals and strategies. Often these are the more frequent type. The best run 1:1 of this type involves less "telling/talking" from the manager and more questions about what's working, what's not working and ways to remove roadblocks. Most managers talk too much and ask too few questions. The second type of 1:1 is more developmentally focused. The best ones start with an understanding of my career goals, ambitions, and expectations. Followed by a conversation on what I/we need to do to make these hopes a reality. It is highly collaborative."

Key Takeaways

- **Four Steps of 1:1s.** There are four key stages of 1:1 meetings: 1) Pre-Start, 2) Start, 3) The Heart, and 4) End. Each step is central to how 1:1s are conducted.
- **The Pre-Start and Start Phases Set the Tone.** The Pre-Start of 1:1s ensures you prepare for the meeting and show up with the right mindset. The Start of the meeting should begin with light topics (such as non-work-related topics, wins, or gratitude) and then dive into heavier topics such as discussing roadblocks or providing feedback.
- **The Heart is Central to 1:1 Effectiveness.** This is the core of the 1:1. Five key phases happen in this phase: 1) Expressing, 2) Clarifying and Understanding, 3) Solutioning, 4) Crafting Next Steps, and 5) Monitoring the Agenda. These phases do not need to happen in a step-by-step manner. Rather, let the conversation flow and proceed through the stages in a manner that makes good sense for the particular agenda topic.

- **End Positively.** The end of the 1:1 is a critical opportunity to review and informally document key takeaways. Always make sure to end on time, with gratitude, a reiteration of your support. These actions will help motivate the direct to take action on what was discussed and will also set your next 1:1 up for success.

11

The Direct's Job During the 1:1 Is to Do What?

Everything in the universe has rhythm. Everything dances.
Maya Angelou

A 1:1 is a dance of sorts—after all, it does take two to tango. There may be one person leading, but clearly, that is not enough. Both parties have a critical role in putting the dance together. Each party shapes the 1:1 and is responsible for its success or failure. The direct does not play a passive role in 1:1s; they play an active role in making these meetings truly effective—in doing so, they help build the relationship and work to get needs met. This chapter is dedicated to the critical behaviors of the direct in boosting 1:1 success, so in this chapter, I speak directly to direct reports. You are the "you" throughout this chapter. However, (and this is a big however) the content is clearly relevant to the manager, as many of the behaviors discussed should still be enacted by managers when leading a 1:1. Furthermore, managers also likely participate in 1:1s with *their* manager, making this chapter even more relevant.

What can, and should, the direct do to maximize 1:1 value and increase the chances of positive outcomes? Ten behaviors emerged quite robustly in my interviews that I want to share. Without further ado: the Terrific 10, the Tremendous 10, the Top 10—the 10 behaviors that take the 1:1 to the top.

#1
Know What You Need

You can't get what you want out of 1:1s unless you first know what you want. What are your top issues and topics to discuss? What are your pressing needs? Don't get bogged down by superficial topics or details, or things you *think* you should talk about. Figure out your meaningful short- and long-term needs, hopes, and goals. Your clarity of purpose helps you prioritize and organize your talking points and questions. This will ultimately increase the chances of the 1:1 truly giving you what you need.

#2
Be Curious

Being curious starts with mindset, but it is also about one's behaviors. It reflects a desire to grow and learn from others and from experiences, to acquire new knowledge, and to wrestle willingly with disparate pieces of information. Research has found curiosity is associated with several positive outcomes such as:

- Higher levels of job performance
- Higher levels of job satisfaction and life satisfaction
- Better and deeper social relationships
- Entrepreneurial behaviors
- Adaptability and growth

While most people would say they are curious by nature, in practice, they don't behave curiously. We go through our days moving at the speed of light. We get distracted by deadlines, social media, and problems. And perhaps most notably, we get in our own way by not truly investing our time in learning from others and their "truths"—a key feature of curiosity. Besides actively cueing yourself to have a curious mindset (yes, we need to remind ourselves of this before going into a 1:1), the basics of curiosity are clear—we are asking questions, listening carefully, and enjoying the process of discovery. Most importantly, perhaps, we are working to avoid confirmation bias (i.e., when we only seek information consistent with our beliefs) and challenging ourselves to discover new knowledge and new ways of thinking even if it makes us uncomfortable. Ultimately, we are learning about others' narratives and truths. While we may not agree with them, they still provide an opportunity to learn and grow.

#3
Build Rapport

Building rapport helps people get to know each other on a personal and professional level and feel comfortable with one another. Building rapport is clearly a dynamic process. Some managers are highly introverted or may be a bit awkward socially, but this does not mean that you can't build rapport. Instead, this just means you must work extra hard to build this relationship and connection. Generally, the literature recommends starting with an enthusiastic, positive greeting. Use nonverbals like good eye contact and a smile to draw the other party in. Take an interest in the other person and who they are. Learn about their passions and interests to find synergies and common ground that can be used to elevate the conversation. When there is not common ground, you can still be curious and take an interest in the differences. Allow the conversation to progress naturally, but engage with what you hear to build momentum. And most importantly, enjoy the process of connecting.

#4
Actively Engage

This is your meeting; get the most out of it. The more obvious examples of engagement are sharing and interacting with content, asking questions, expressing yourself, being forthcoming, reacting constructively to what is said, probing, clarifying, and being fully present. Taking notes can also foster and signal engagement. Additionally, because the meeting involves just two parties, nonverbal communication is highly apparent and even more impactful on interpersonal dynamics. Sitting up, leaning slightly forward, smiling, and making eye contact are strong positive nonverbal signals of engagement.

#5
Communicate Well

Let me highlight a few key behaviors associated with excellent communication.

- **Be clear and concise.** Use accessible and precise vocabulary to prevent miscommunications.
- **Communication is like telling a story.** A good structure, flow, and organization is essential.
- **Stay focused and stick to your message.** Jumping around will confuse your listener.
- **Your voice matters.** Inflection and tone influence how communication is received. These two communication elements affect understanding and interpretation of messages.
- **Be honest.** To increases the chances of a meaningful and thoughtful response, work to be honest, candid, and even vulnerable with your manager.

And remember, the cornerstone of great communication is listening (see Chapter 9). I do want to add, unless confidential or highly sensitive, it may be useful at times to practice your communication on a difficult issue or topic with a trusted colleague to better prepare you for having a potentially difficult conversation with your manager.

#6
Problem Solve

Don't just come to 1:1s with your problems, try to also come with potential solutions to those problems, even if half-baked. This will signal your proactiveness and desire to constructively tackle challenges. Be willing to share your point of view, even if it differs from your manager's. If disagreements or conflicts arise, work through the differences constructively. Remember, differences between parties is not an issue per se, it is just an opportunity to learn different perspectives. The key is talking through them in a way that is not attacking or personal. And resolving differences can yield unique and integrative solutions.

Related to this, let me share some of the learning from the excellent work of Baldoni on defending ideas without being defensive.[1] It starts with preparation. Think about the types of objections and counterarguments you might receive around your ideas and brainstorm some potential responses. This is not designed to entrench you in defending your points at all costs, but it increases the chances of your ideas getting full attention and can promote thoughtful deliberation. It may also help you discover holes in your argument before the conversation starts. During the meeting itself, if you get pushback, express appreciation (not necessarily agreement) with any feedback or response you receive. This serves as a signal of your open-mindedness and receptivity, which in turn can make others more open-minded. It also makes conversations more pleasant, which can result in less entrenchment. Patience is also key. Be realistic with how quickly someone will embrace your perspective. Related, be open to refining your ideas in response to feedback. Identify what is core to your proposal and what is superficial. Don't hesitate to yield on the superficial as it can build momentum. Finally, keep your cool. If you get emotional, the conversation can take a turn for the worse.

It certainly can be the case that during the discussion, it becomes apparent that your ideas do have some problems and that an alternative path is warranted. Or it could be the case that you just can't bring the other party on board. That happens. It is not reasonable to expect others to always be swayed by your arguments. Sometimes you just must move forward and pivot. But, if the process is handled well, this whole experience will reflect well on you.

#7
Ask for Help (Constructively)

Seeking help from others is crucial when taking on new challenges, confronting obstacles, working under pressure to meet deadlines, and disentangling nebulous tasks and expectations. Consequently, scholars have studied help-seeking behaviors, particularly in the last two decades. Help-seeking behaviors have been categorized by social psychologists into two main types: autonomous help-seeking and dependent help-seeking.[2] Autonomous help-seeking can be understood as seeking information that enables individuals to be independent, accomplish tasks, and solve problems on their own. This tends to promote long-term independence—similar to the adage, "Give a person a fish and they'll eat for a day but teach them to fish and they'll eat for a lifetime." Dependent help-seeking, on the other hand, refers to searching for a "quick fix" and an "answer" from someone else. This style of help-seeking conserves time and effort and leads to immediate gratification, but typically doesn't yield long-term self-sufficiency. Interestingly, job performance ratings have been shown to have a positive relationship with autonomous help-seeking, but a negative relationship with its counterpart—dependent help-seeking.[3]

I recognize that asking for help is not always an easy thing to do. However, it is made easier if you have a track record of offering help to others. In fact, you can ask many of the questions discussed in Chapter 6, tweaked to focus on the manager, as a way of learning what is on their mind and how you might be able to help them. For example, you can ask your manager: "What are your priorities over the next X days and what can I do to help you with this?" An offer of help from you will surely be well received, although it is not the primary purpose of the 1:1. It is a nice thing to do and can increases the chances of others stepping up to help you (helping begets helping).

#8
Ask for Feedback

When seeking out feedback, it's useful to be targeted and specific. Here are some good questions you can ask your manager to gain helpful counsel:

- What am I doing well and what can I improve on?
- What are my strengths and where can I develop more?
- Where are my blind spots when it comes to (*insert a work topic*)?
- What additional knowledge or skills would make me more effective in this role?
- What advice would you have for me to excel and advance in this organization?
- Where do you see my future as being with your team and the organization?
- To get to where I want to be from a career perspective, what knowledge/skills do I need to work on and further develop?

Additionally, it can be helpful to follow up with "and, what else?" after you've received feedback. This allows your manager to reflect and add anything they might have missed.

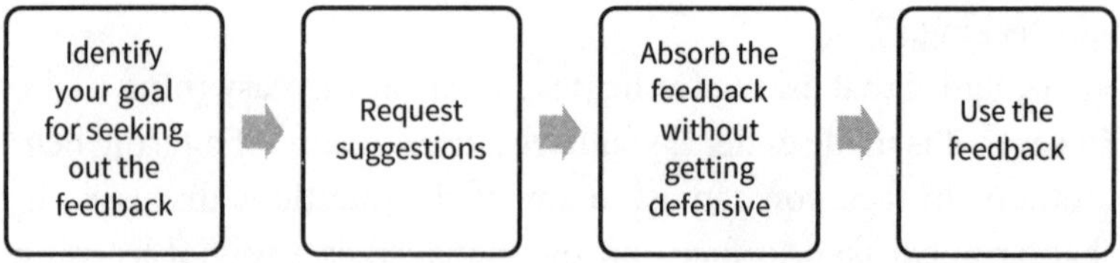

I also encourage you to embrace the feedforward concept noted earlier, a terrific approach pioneered by Marshall Goldsmith.[4] This approach focuses on future behaviors rather than focusing on what went wrong in the past. Feedforward is designed to be nonjudgmental, empowering, and insightful. This can happen in a four-step process:

1. **Identify your goal for seeking out the feedback.** What behavior, generally under your control, is one that you like to get better at. Or, what behavior do you feel hinders your ability to thrive and/or other's ability to thrive and succeed. This could include behaviors associated with teamwork, personal productivity, elevating others, promoting your well-being, addressing a work–life issue, dealing with difficult people, resolving conflicts or tense situations, managing workloads, fostering more innovation, etc. Once you identify the behavior(s), clearly communicate that you would like to get better at XYZ and describe the reason behind the desire to be sure it is clear.
2. **Request suggestions.** Focus on future-oriented solutions and make *no* references to the past. Here are some examples: "I would like to get better at prioritization, what are your suggestions on how to get better at this behavior?" or "I want to improve my skills at resolving conflicts among team members, what do you think are the best ways of doing that?" or "I am fascinated by how some people handle stress so well, what do you see as the keys for managing stress on the job?" To make this go smoothly, it may be best to simply ask the other party for two suggestions, which makes the task more manageable. This whole process can take just 2–3 minutes.
3. **Absorb the feedback without getting defensive.** Listen to what the other person has to say. Probe to understand, but not debate. You can ask for clarity, but don't evaluate their solutions with them—just say "thank you for the suggestions." In the end, they are just suggestions, and you will ultimately decide what positive changes you try to make.

4. **Use the feedback.** Take notes on what you learned, reflect on them, then seek out new behaviors to try. Chapter 13 has additional content on making positive behavioral changes.

Feedforward assessments give insight into how a situation can be improved in the future rather than focusing on positive or negative past behaviors. After all, we can't change the past, but we can change the future. Feedforward is nonjudgmental, empowering, and eye-opening. What makes feedforward so powerful is that while people often dread getting feedback, people are generally excited to give and receive feedforward. This is because feedforward is an optimistic effort focusing on solutions instead of problems. Relatedly, feedforward does not elicit defensiveness as you are discussing a future path forward rather than a past incident. This yields suggestions for you to consider, rather than edicts to enact or corrections to make. Overall, feedforward is all about possibilities for positive change. It helps the person grow and develop without the negative tension that hearing feedback around past behaviors can have. Even more so, everyone can benefit greatly from feedforward. In fact, most people even describe the process as uplifting and fun.

The bonus of feedforward is that you can apply the practice outside of the 1:1 meeting or even the work environment. The only requirement is that whoever you ask should have familiarity with the growth area more broadly. Even family and friends are positioned to do this if desired.

#9
Receive Feedback Well

Sometimes hearing negative feedback can be challenging, even if you're open to receiving it. While it can be distressing to hear, there's actually a way to train yourself to view all kinds of feedback as an extremely helpful tool. Those who are really adept at receiving feedback—good or bad—begin by thanking the feedback giver for sharing. Next, they ask probing questions to gain further insight into the issue being raised. They also know that not everyone is great at communicating feedback and that how feedback is delivered can vary. However, they continue to have an overall appreciation of what feedback can offer. Relatedly, they avoid speaking when agitated, because it can make things spiral in a bad direction. It's also important to note that receiving feedback doesn't mean you have to address every single thing you heard. The next chapter discusses a process for making progress on actions and working to manage the perceptions of others toward your efforts, including when receiving feedback.

#10
Express Gratitude

Last, show gratitude for your manager's time and advice. Even if you are not 100% on board with all that was discussed, we can certainly find reasons for gratitude. This elevates you as a person (being a grateful person is crucial for well-being) and can improve your relationship with your manager. When expressing gratitude, here are some points to keep in mind.

#1	It is ok to be a little hyperbolic as it displays enthusiasm. For example, "this is going to be incredibly helpful—thank you" or "I can't thank you enough for all that you have done here."
#2	Try to be specific where you can, in order to make the gratitude even more salient. For example, "I greatly appreciate the perspective you shared on X."
#3	Don't forget to make eye contact and smile when sharing your gratitude.
#4	Mix up how you convey gratitude, so it is more noticeable.
#5	You can express your emotions as part of the gratitude. For example, "your support means the world to me" or "I feel incredibly seen and heard—thank you."

Overall, the 10 behaviors described in this chapter are about you doing your part in making your 1:1s successful. Your manager's behaviors are absolutely critical, but your house is only in order if you also effectively execute your part. At the same time, these behaviors reflect well on you as a person and should lead to more positive impressions of you by your manager. Before closing the chapter, I want to cover a special topic—providing feedback to your manager.

Do I Give Feedback to My Manager?

Let me start by sharing three musings meant to entertain, but they do contain kernels of truth when answering this question.

> *"Feedback is such a gift, unless someone doesn't want it."*
>
> *"Giving feedback can really build a relationship, unless they think you are flat out wrong."*
>
> *"People will want to hear your thoughts, unless they think you suck."*

To give solicited or unsolicited feedback to someone in a position of more power is quite a tricky effort, but it can be done. Furthermore, when it is done well it can lead to positive outcomes for both you and the manager. First, it is important to determine whether you are making a mountain out of a molehill. Spend time thinking about whether the situation in question warrants a conversation and feedback. Next, ask yourself if the situation will naturally resolve itself. If you still think it will be useful feedback for your manager to hear, ask yourself if the potential costs outweigh the potential benefits. In other words, how important is this to you? One way to gauge this is to observe how your manager responds to feedback, such as how they responded to feedback from others or you in the past. Were they open to it? Or were they defensive? If all seems worth pursuing, here is a potential process to tailor to your style.

Preparation for Feedback Giving

- Give your manager a heads-up about hoping to communicate feedback to them to prime the conversation, prevent them from feeling blindsided, and pave the way to a constructive conversation.
- Think carefully about their potential responses to your feedback. Think through what you want to say in response. Preparation is key.
- Remember that there is likely more context to the situation than you're fully aware of. For example, there might be pressure from shareholders that is influencing your manager's decisions.
- Practice what you want to say. This will allow you to focus on the task at hand when the time comes and to deliver your feedback in the clearest way possible without being too distracted by your nerves.

How to Execute Respectfully, Thoughtfully, and Constructively

- Proceed with agreement. In other words, start the conversation by asking if they are still open to hearing some feedback on X.
- Begin by expressing gratitude for them being open to your feedback and state your intentions. Frame your feedback in a constructive and helpful way.
- Identify the situation that you're providing feedback about.
- Explain your perspective of the specific behavior(s).
- Describe the impact that their behavior(s) are having on you, if relevant.
- Point out specific ways that their behavior(s) might be inhibiting goals, if relevant.
- Have your focus be on how you can help your manager improve, rather than what you would do differently if you were in their shoes.

- When the conversation is ending, remember to thank your manager for being open to hearing your concerns and being receptive to feedback. If applicable, you can also offer support to help them address the feedback you shared.

Once you've finished delivering your feedback, pause and allow your manager enough time to digest your message and respond accordingly. This requires some patience. In the case that your manager is defensive and/or angry, it's helpful to apologize for the impact of your feedback (the way it made them think and feel—e.g., "I'm sorry this has upset you"), remind them of your intention, and ask clarifying questions if needed.

Key Takeaways

- **1:1s are a Dance.** Directs play an active role in making 1:1s work.
- **The 10 Direct Behaviors that are Critical.** You (directs) need to take an active role in your 1:1s to get the most out of them. Ten key behaviors are critical in this respect: 1) Know What You Need, 2) Be Curious, 3) Build Rapport, 4) Actively Engage, 5) Communicate Well, 6) Problem Solve, 7) Ask for Help (Constructively), 8) Ask for Feedback, 9) Receive Feedback Well, and 10) Express Gratitude.
- **These Behaviors are Also Relevant for Managers.** While you (directs) should enact these behaviors to increase the effectiveness of their 1:1s, they are also relevant for managers. For example, managers need to be actively engaged in 1:1s too.
- **Directs Can Give Feedback, but in a Considerate Way.** While it may seem daunting to do, you and your manager can benefit from providing upward feedback. However, it's important for you to go about it in a thoughtful way. Make sure to prime your manager of your desire to give them feedback. When giving feedback, be respectful, thoughtful, and constructive so that managers are more likely to take the feedback less defensively.

Section 2 Tools

Two tools are presented next to help you carry out your 1:1s, which include:

1. Preparation Checklist for 1:1 Facilitation
2. True/False Quiz on Skills for Dealing with Negative Emotions in 1:1s

Preparation Checklist for 1:1 Facilitation

This tool serves as a reminder checklist for facilitating your 1:1s.

Effective Facilitation: Key Behaviors		
Category	**Key Behaviors**	
Expressing	• Start positively to get your direct talking.	[ ]
	• Follow up on previous action items at the start of the 1:1.	[ ]
	• Show appreciation for your direct's perspective.	[ ]
	• Use appropriate body language and eye contact.	[ ]
	• Manage the climate to build trust.	[ ]
	• Motivate, empower, support, and inspire directs.	[ ]
	• Encourage open dialogue.	[ ]
Clarifying & Understanding	• Paraphrase what you hear.	[ ]
	• Stay neutral during decision-making.	[ ]
	• Actively listen so your directs feel heard and understood.	[ ]
	• Follow up on questions to create clarity on motives.	[ ]
	• Synthesize you and your direct's ideas.	[ ]
	• Ask questions to get to root causes.	[ ]

Effective Facilitation: Key Behaviors		
Category	**Key Behaviors**	
Solutioning	• Gently test/challenge your direct's assumptions.	[ ]
	• Provide general counsel, support, suggestions, and advice.	[ ]
	• Work collaboratively on problems.	[ ]
	• Identify available support and resources for your direct.	[ ]
	• Allow directs to problem solve first, then offer suggestions.	[ ]
	• Lean into silence in the 1:1.	[ ]
Crafting Next Steps	• Record ideas by taking notes.	[ ]
	• Communicate clear expectations for next action items.	[ ]
	• Ensure action items are specific, achievable, and time-bound.	[ ]
	• Summarize key discussion points.	[ ]
	• Establish action items at the end of the 1:1.	[ ]
	• Make certain action items are agreed upon.	[ ]
	• Follow up on action items after the 1:1 for accountability.	[ ]

Effective Facilitation: Key Behaviors		
Category	**Key Behaviors**	
Monitoring the Agenda	• Start with high-priority agenda items.	[ ]
	• Use the agenda, but don't use it as a crutch.	[ ]
	• Be flexible to what your direct wants to talk about.	[ ]
	• Ensure key points are discussed.	[ ]
	• Keep discussion on track.	[ ]
	• Assess timing so meeting ends on time.	[ ]
	• Move agenda items not addressed to the next 1:1.	[ ]
	• Discuss agenda items not discussed offline if necessary.	[ ]
	• End meetings with gratitude.	[ ]
With all behaviors, do the following:		
Listen and respond with empathy.		[ ]
Communicate authentically and transparently.		[ ]
Involve directs appropriately.		[ ]
Be kind and supportive.		[ ]
Demonstrate appropriate vulnerability.		[ ]

True/False Quiz on Skills for Dealing with Negative Emotions in 1:1s

Sometimes, negative emotions, such as anger, can arise in 1:1s. However, there are things you can do to effectively handle these difficult but inevitable situations. This tool tests your knowledge on how to do so.

Directions:

Below is a list of statements for handling anger and negative emotions in 1:1s. Go through each item and circle whether you think the statement is true or false. Once you're done, check your answers in the answer key on the next page.

True/False Quiz:

True or false, when dealing with anger and/or negative emotions in 1:1s you should . . .	True or False?	Correct?
1. Try to get your direct to explain why they're angry.	[T/F]	
2. Give your opinion right away.	[T/F]	
3. Let your direct know right away when you disagree with their perspective.	[T/F]	
4. Actively listen to your direct's perspective.	[T/F]	
5. Immediately express your thoughts about why you think they are wrong.	[T/F]	
6. Encourage your direct to explain how they feel.	[T/F]	
7. Communicate how you didn't appreciate their angry response.	[T/F]	

True or false, when dealing with anger and/or negative emotions in 1:1s you should . . .	True or False?	Correct?
8. React immediately with how you feel in the moment.	[T/F]	
9. Avoid asking questions to dive deeper into the issue.	[T/F]	
10. Empathize with your direct's perspective on the situation.	[T/F]	
11. Address the issue right away, even if your direct is still angry.	[T/F]	
12. Take responsibility and apologize for your role in the situation.	[T / F]	
Total Correct. ______		

Answer Key

Below are the answers to each of the true and false statements. Use the list and put a checkmark next to each that you got correct. Then, total your number of checkmarks at the bottom of the far-right column.

1.	True	7.	True
2.	False	8.	False
3.	False	9.	False
4.	True	10.	True
5.	False	11.	False
6.	True	12.	True

Interpretation

- 10–12 Correct. Excellent work! Keep using these skills to deal with these challenging 1:1 situations.
- 7–9 Correct. Nice job! Review the answers you got incorrect to help you deal with these challenging 1:1 situations even more effectively.
- 0–6 Correct. Review the answers you got incorrect and use the content of the book to help you navigate these 1:1 situations more effectively.

SECTION 3

AFTER THE MEETING

This section of the book discusses what happens after the 1:1 in terms of what needs to be done to cement success and get the full value of these meetings. Then we turn to how to evaluate 1:1s and determine if they are truly making a difference and what needs to change to make them work optimally for all parties.

> *1:1s between a manager and their directs are probably the primary and most important way to build a mutually satisfying relationship. This is core to leadership success. Without such a relationship, trust suffers, and along with it, team members' willingness to get behind and follow the lead of the manager in a deep and genuine way.*
>
> Executive, Trane Technologies

> *1:1s are all about fostering a meaningful human connection. These meetings can have tremendous effects on how your team experiences you as a leader, the work they do, and their relationship with the organization. It can make or break a person's day, week, or even a year. There is potentially nothing more important than the 1:1 meeting. The long-term impact of these personal moments is tremendous and should be taken very seriously.*
>
> Executive, Deloitte

12

The Meeting Is Done, Now What?

Picture this situation. Two employees—Jamel and Dave—both report to Rosario. One day, they both have 1:1s. Jamel comes out of his 1:1 with a plan of action. He then fulfils his commitments. Dave also comes out of his 1:1 with a plan of action. However, he does not fulfill his commitments. All too often when trying to explain these two opposite patterns of behavior, we would simply conclude that Jamel is motivated while Dave is not. Jamel is a go-getter, and Dave is lazy. Jamel has a bright future ahead of him, and Dave does not. However, looking at research on why commitments are often not kept sheds a more nuanced light going beyond the simple reasoning that Jamel is good, and Dave is bad.

Here are seven interrelated reasons to better understand why commitments are not met. In this case, we will use Dave as an example.

Reason 1	Dave was not committed to the action in question.
Reason 2	Dave may have met the commitment in his eyes, but others may not see it that way.
Reason 3	Dave forgot what he committed to.
Reason 4	Dave did not have time to address the commitment.
Reason 5	Dave did not prioritize the commitment.
Reason 6	Dave found he doesn't have agency/skills/ability to carry out the commitment.
Reason 7	Something got in the way of Dave carrying out the commitment.

Several observations emerge when looking at this diverse set of explanations. First, reason #1 should hopefully be irrelevant if the 1:1 (where the action item emerged from) is carried out in a way such that personal needs are truly met. Namely, if the direct feels listened to, respected, and is genuinely involved in solutioning, their buy-in to commitments should be quite high. The rest of the reasons fall into two main categories: a lack of clarity that limits success (reasons #2 and #3) and personal/situational issues that limit success (reasons #4–7). Good news, there are ways to remove these derailers. The behaviors shared below are relevant to your personal efforts to carry out your own commitments and can also serve as counsel that you can share with your directs to help them with their actions.

Creating Clarity

Clarity of commitments is greatly promoted through shared documentation. To do so, finalize and distribute 1:1 notes (not full meeting minutes) within 24–48 hours after the meeting. While both parties should take notes during the meeting, one person should send out a post-meeting summary. This responsibility can be rotated. Then, the other person can update if needed, culminating into a final draft. The notes typically have two primary pieces, one optional and one required:

Optional:	Summaries of the conversation around each agenda item
Required:	A list of action items (including support actions), specifying who is doing what and a timeline of expectations/deadlines.

Here is an example of something that could get distributed after a 1:1:

Our 1:1 on August 28th, 2023

Jane@company.com

Our 1:1 on August 28th, 2023

Jane,

It was really great meeting with you today. Here is what I took away from our discussion. Please take a moment to reflect on the meeting and let me know what I missed or what needs to be changed:

- I will get you the regional forecast data by the end of the week
- You will send me an updated project management schedule by next Monday. Most importantly, you will indicate places you need me to jump in
- I look forward to hearing how your presentation to marketing goes. I really liked the ideas we discussed
- Please let me know if I can help you as you work to resolve that conflict between Sasha and Gordon. I hope the strategy we discussed works as we hope. If desired, I am happy to send you our internal learning module on conflict resolution. Let me know
- On the career development front, you will pick one training program to keep you on track for developing the skills needed for your desired progression
- Thanks for letting me know about the elder care dilemma you are facing. Please let me know how I can support you when needed.

Have a great day,
Maria
The Manager

This type of documentation, once finalized, serves as a contract of sorts, getting everyone on the same page. It promotes accountability and increases the chances of positive action happening. This documentation is also helpful for future meeting preparation and follow-up as it can be consulted when creating the next 1:1 agenda. Relatedly, these notes serve as an archive of the journey of the team member (especially the tracking of themes and issues over time), which could be extremely useful when needing to do formal personnel actions such as performance reviews, promotions, and new assignments.

In research with my fantastic doctoral student, Jack Flinchum, note-taking in 1:1s among managers was positively associated with directs' evaluation of the manager's overall effectiveness. Why might that correlation exist? We postulate that the manager that takes notes in 1:1s is a manager who takes 1:1s more seriously; they are more motivated to act on what was agreed upon and are more inclined to support their directs. These behaviors likely make the manager more effective in the eyes of their team members, even outside of the 1:1s. Furthermore, managers who take notes during 1:1s likely come across to the direct as more present, motivated, and committed to the direct.

Motivating Action and Overcoming Personal and Situational Issues

The consequences of not keeping a commitment are significant. First, the obvious, unfilled commitments can undermine progress and effectiveness. Second, failing to fulfill a commitment hurts the reputation and standing of the person not doing what they said they would do. This person is essentially mortgaging their name, which could serve to ultimately derail them from progressing in their career. To increase the chances of fulfilling commitments and to stay motivated in doing so, consider the three actions I unpack in the next paragraph. These actions are designed to increase motivation, but also to provide additional counsel to help traverse obstacles.

First, have an accountability partner. Share what you have committed to with someone else (e.g., a peer, a friend, a partner). This implicitly increases pressure for you to act and follow through on your commitment. The accountability partner can also provide advice, counsel, and support as needed to help with progress and overcoming challenges. Check in with them regularly. Doing so will keep you motivated. Second, actually schedule time to fulfill the commitment. We typically do what is scheduled. Therefore, carve out time in a day, multiple days, or multiple weeks to work on meeting your commitment. Just like how you would rarely miss a meeting on your calendar, schedule time to work toward your commitment to increase the chances of you fulfilling it. Third, if you are having trouble getting motivated to work toward fulfilling the commitment, start small to build momentum. Make some progress to encourage more progress.[1] You can even chart progress to increase focus and seeing your progress can be motivating.

To help drive change and progress, consider trying the daily question approach discussed by a mentor of mine, Marshall Goldsmith, to drive change.[2] Create a spreadsheet containing the key behaviors/actions you are working on, framed as questions. For example, "Did I do my best today to communicate with my remote employees?"; "Did I do my best today to win back lapsed customers?"; "Did I do my best today to respond to emails in a timely way?"; "Did I do my best today to try to avoid proving I was right when it wasn't worth it?" For each of these questions, give yourself a score each day (the columns of the spreadsheet are organized by date). Answer these questions daily, without fail (I do mine at 8 p.m. each night). This allows you to keep what you are working on top of mind, and you can chart your progress. If you are not making the desired progress, analyze it, bring in support as needed, and keep working on it.

Marshall Goldsmith shared some client reactions in his research on this approach.[3] Here is one such reaction that captures how many respondents felt: "After a few days, when I knew I would be answering the survey later in the day, I attempted to shape my day and become more purposeful in my interactions with others and more thoughtful about how I spent my time." Having a day filled with perfect scores is not realistic. There will be hiccups throughout the process. But overall, this approach energizes action and change in meeting your goals. To push for progress even more, consider giving yourself simple rewards (e.g., a break, a treat, a desired activity) for making progress on your commitment.

There is an additional technique I learned from Marshall that helps drive change and promotes changing the perceptions of key stakeholders: when the actions we are addressing are people-focused, we want those around us to notice what we are doing. We want others to see that we are engaged and trying to be our best selves. This creates empathy so that when we do have slip-ups (which are inevitable), others give us the benefit of the doubt rather than just thinking, "There he goes again, Dave just doesn't care." Here is what this looks like:

#1	Identify some key stakeholders—those that connect with or are affected by the action you are working on.
#2	For each stakeholder (or subset of them), tell them what you are working on.
#3	Ask them for advice for making progress for, say, the first two months.
#4	After this timeframe, check in with them to see how things went. Ask them for additional advice for the next two months.
#5	Check in with them after the two months—keep repeating this process.

These actions help others see what you are doing, understand your efforts and dedication, and make these stakeholders part of your "change team." All of this, in concert with their counsel, increases the chances of action happening and people noticing.

If you just can't make it work and wind up breaking a commitment, own up to it. Apologize to the parties affected. Explain what happened, ask how you can remedy the situation, and work toward making sure it does not happen again.

Following Up/Accountability

Until now I have focused on the commitments of one person in the 1:1 meeting. But there are two parties in 1:1s, and it is usually the case that both parties have made commitments. If you have done your action item(s) but the other party in the 1:1 has not, here are some ideas on how to follow up to prompt their action.

1. Communicate your progress and completion to the other party. This typically will get the other party moving, as it creates positive pressure to act, but not always. Reminders may be needed.
2. Remind the other party, but not every day. Use a nonaggressive cadence. Some find it helpful to put on their calendar times to check in with the other person, so they don't forget.
3. Keep reminders on the same email stream so all can be found in one place.
4. Reach out through other means if needed, such as stopping by their office.
5. Change the content of each reminder/nudge. Add new information, details, or questions so that the nudge feels less like nagging.
6. Be empathetic and courteous in your communications, such as by saying, "I know you are busy. . . ." Brevity, warmth, and empathy for the other person's schedule are better received than just a terse reminder. Consider phrases like: "Just a gentle nudge . . ."; "A friendly prompt. . . ."

Once the other party completes the action, express your appreciation and gratitude. If commitments are still not being completed after prompting, this can be probed and explored in a future 1:1 to better understand the situation and potential constraints. By allowing room for more context, rather than just blaming or getting angry, you are giving the other person the benefit of the doubt and it communicates that you're empathetic of competing demands. You can position yourself as a resource. Finally, the beauty of regular and frequent 1:1s is that the accountability is built in naturally—the other party likely does not need to be nudged outside of the meeting if they don't complete the actions they committed to as it can be part of the next 1:1 discussion which is just around the corner. Let me close by referring you to two key checklists at the end of this book section that will help you give and receive feedback, but also promote action and foster accountability.

Key Takeaways

- **Follow Through on Commitments.** After the meeting ends, it is critical for both you and your directs to follow through on the action items they committed to. Breaking commitments hurts trust, hurts the working relationship, and makes it harder to have effective 1:1s in the future.
- **Broken Commitments Are Usually Avoidable.** There are many reasons why commitments are broken, and they are often not because the person avoided accomplishing the task. For example, action items may be unclear or there may be personal/situational derailers for accomplishing the commitment.
- **Set Commitments Up Effectively.** Several tactics can be used to make sure commitments are kept. Focus on creating clarity of what the action item is so people understand what they are to accomplish. Find ways to spark motivation and reduce barriers to success. Follow up with the other person on their progress and your own progress.

13
Did the 1:1 Work?

Answer quickly, which line is longer, the top or the bottom?

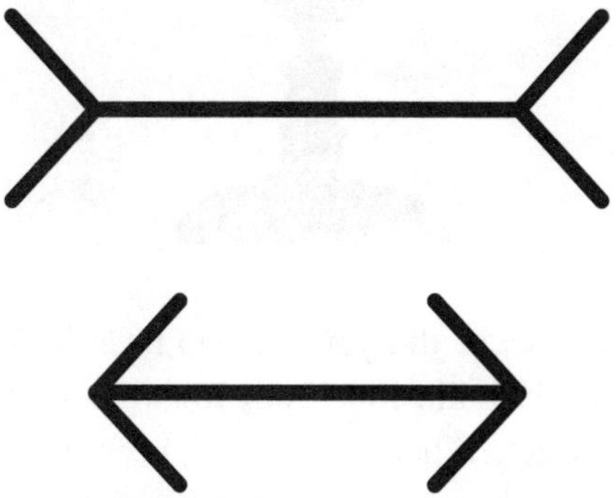

Answer quickly again, which dot is bigger, the one on the left or the one on the right?

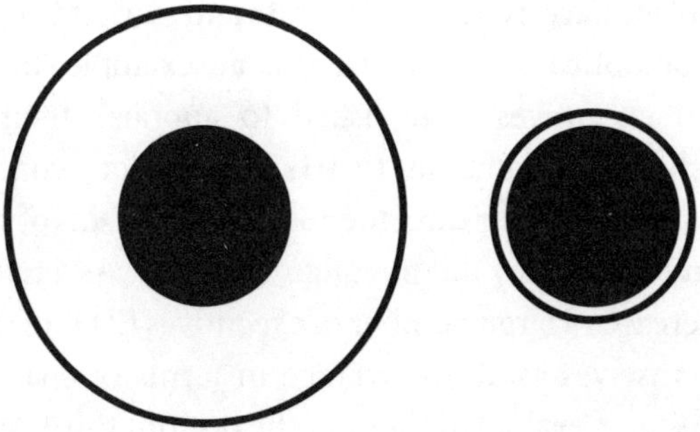

Curious as to the answers? The lines are the same length in the first, and the dots are the same size in the second. Most people think the lines and dots are different sizes, because our brains trick us. Our perceptions are often inaccurate. Yet we feel quite confident in them as we are "seeing" it with our own eyes. Here's another example. Glance at this picture, what do you see?

Did you see a vase, or did you see two faces looking at one another? In this optical illusion, both answers—while completely different—are correct. What we perceive becomes our truth. And that truth influences how we understand the world around us and our behaviors. Let me bring this back to 1:1s. Knowing whether a 1:1 is truly working as we had hoped can be quite challenging. The main problem is that our self-perception, the most readily available assessment tool we have, is quite inaccurate and subject to distortion—just like these optical illusions. Here is an example. In one study, nearly 4,000 executives were asked to appraise their coaching skills—which are fundamental to 1:1s. The leaders' coaching skills were also assessed by their direct reports. The two sets of scores were then compared, and they did not align very well. As a rather jarring example, there was a large number of executives (24% of the sample) that saw themselves as above average in terms of coaching skills, while their directs evaluated them in the bottom third. What a dramatic difference! As psychology professor David Myers discusses, there is a robust human tendency to overestimate our knowledge, skills, abilities, and personality traits relative to others.[1] Interestingly, this effect applies to many aspects of life, from assessing one's driving skills to judging one's intelligence. We just aren't as accurate as we think—we often think we are better than we are.

Overall, you may think your 1:1s are going well, but your direct may have other opinions. Given this, when reflecting on the quality of our 1:1s we need to make efforts to guard against an inflated positive bias of how effective our 1:1s are. Here are three ways to do just that:

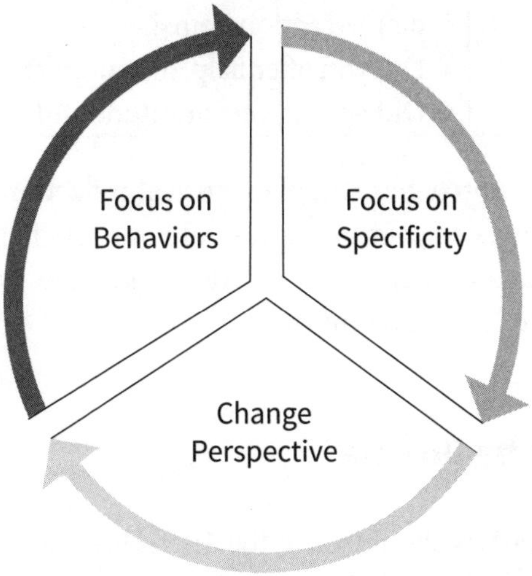

Strategy	Description
Focus on Specificity	Instead of a general reflection, challenge yourself to identify three specific moments/behaviors that went well and three specific moments/behaviors that did not go well.
Change Perspective	Take the perspective of the other party, and reflect on the 1:1 while "in their shoes." What would your direct say are three things that went well and three things that did not go well? What would your direct say are three ways the 1:1 could become more valuable?

Strategy	Description
Focus on Behaviors	Focus your reflection on behaviors. Some examples: • Did you engage in active listening techniques? • Did you listen more than you spoke? • Did you ask your direct for ideas and suggestions? • Did you and/or your direct leave with well-defined action items? • Did you offer help and support? • Did you express gratitude and appreciation?

These three approaches stimulate critical reflection and can decrease the chances of your perception of your 1:1s being distorted. Do this periodically after 1:1s. It will only take a few minutes, but it will push you to learn and improve.

Evaluation by Directs

Ideally, both parties should leave the 1:1 feeling valued, respected, supported, and informed about next steps, solutions, and agreed-upon commitments. However, in many regards, your feelings coming out of 1:1s are irrelevant. This is because 1:1s, by definition, are meetings for the direct. In this way, the direct's feelings about the value of their 1:1s is the critical criterion for 1:1 success. Did the direct indeed find the 1:1 valuable in meeting their practical and personal needs? If so, the 1:1 was successful. If not, the 1:1 was not as successful as it could have been. Don't get me wrong, there could be critical feedback for (in)actions given to directs that occur in the 1:1. But, when delivered effectively, the practical and personal needs of the direct can still be met in these situations. Also, note that I am not defining success as happiness and joy following the meeting per se—although that is certainly a bonus and absolutely nice to experience. Rather, the goal is to make 1:1s valuable for directs by meeting their needs.

To improve your 1:1s over time, start by asking each direct for their feedback and ideas. This could be done periodically either during, or at the end of a 1:1.

Questions could be:

#1	What was the most useful part of our conversation today?
#2	Did you find value in this 1:1? Why or why not?
#3	What could I do differently to make our 1:1s better for you?

Given potential apprehension, another approach is to anonymously survey all of your directs about what is going well, not so well, and ideas for improvement regarding 1:1s. You can also ask them to assess the overall value of their 1:1s on a five-point scale and then have an open-ended question where they explain their rating. If themes emerge in the data, try new tactics. Your willingness to tweak and experiment with your 1:1s is key. And, if your experiments do not work after say, three months, then gather feedback, reflect why they did not work, and plan your next time-limited experiment(s) until some reasonable success is found.

Lagging Indicators of Success

1:1s clearly influence short-term outcomes, but can influence long-term outcomes as well. Although longer-term indicators are influenced by a host of external factors outside of just 1:1s, they should trend in a positive direction if 1:1s are frequent and effective. Here are a set of long-term indicators to reflect on:

Questions:	Yes/No
Is overall employee engagement in your team improving?	Y/N
Are productivity and retention/turnover metrics across team members trending in a positive direction?	Y/N

Questions:	Yes/No
Are employee performance appraisals improving over time?	Y/N
Are your directs being promoted to the jobs they were aspiring to hold?	Y/N
Are your directs' evaluation of you as a manager improving over time?	Y/N

Overall, 1:1s are an investment of time, resources, and money. Like any investment, 1:1s should be evaluated in a multifaceted way over time. What works at one time for your 1:1s may not work two months later, and what works for one direct may not work for another. Even if you think your current approach is working, do try new things to keep your 1:1s fresh and engaging.

Key Takeaways

- **Our Perceptions of 1:1s Can Be Skewed.** Our minds are powerful. They can work with and against us. Just like in the optical illusions, how effective we see our 1:1s as can be a bit biased. You may think your 1:1s are going great, but your direct may think they are subpar.
- **Apply Strategies to Align Perspectives.** Several strategies can be used to fact-check the inflated view of the effectiveness of your 1:1s that you may have. When reflecting on your 1:1s, identify specific areas that are going well and not well. Take the perspective of your direct when gauging whether your meetings are effective. Last, focus on your specific behaviors during the meetings and how they may support or hinder 1:1 effectiveness.
- **Ask Your Direct for Their Perspective.** By now, you know 1:1s are inherently for your direct. Therefore, the value of 1:1s comes from their perception of whether the meetings are going well. Ask them for feedback and their thoughts on how your 1:1s are

going. Take the feedback, make some changes, see how they work over time, and then reassess.

- **Lagging Indicators Exist.** The best way to see the long-term success of your 1:1s and their effectiveness is with various lagging indicators. For example, are your engagement numbers for the team going up? Is performance rising and turnover dropping? Are directs being promoted to new roles? These long-term factors can be supported by effective 1:1s, which are an investment into your people, your team, and your organization.

Section 3 Tools

Two tools are presented below that are relevant to both Section 2 and 3 of the book. I share both here as they ultimately are designed to promote accountability and change—thus increasing the chances of action happening following the 1:1 and ultimately making the 1:1 most valuable.

1. Checklist for Effectively Giving Feedback & Establishing Accountability in 1:1s
2. Checklist for Effectively Receiving & Acting on Feedback in 1:1s

Checklist for Effectively Giving Feedback & Establishing Accountability in 1:1s

This tool serves as a reminder checklist for giving feedback to your directs and holding them accountable for acting on the feedback. Review each item and make a checkmark next to each. Then, use these behaviors to increase the effectiveness of the feedback process.

Feedback Stage	Key Behaviors	
Direct Asks for Feedback (If Applicable)	• Be open to the request and always agree to provide feedback.	[ ]
	• Ask your direct what they specifically want feedback on.	[ ]
	• Inquire about how your direct prefers the feedback to be delivered.	[ ]
	• Thank your direct for being brave in asking for feedback.	[ ]
	• Probe into what led your direct to want the feedback.	[ ]
Ask to Give Feedback	• Ask if you can give your direct feedback if not asked for.	[ ]
	• Explain the feedback is meant to support not punish them.	[ ]
Give Feedback	• Provide the feedback in a respectful way.	[ ]
	• Speak succinctly when giving the feedback.	[ ]
	• Be specific with your feedback.	[ ]
	• Focus on future behaviors (feedforward).	[ ]
	• Explain how the feedback can help your direct in the future.	[ ]

Feedback Stage	Key Behaviors	
Direct Thinks	• Give your direct time to think about your feedback.	[ ]
	• Do not speak while they are thinking.	[ ]
	• Remind yourself that silence is okay.	[ ]
Direct Responds	• Actively listen to what they have to say about the feedback.	[ ]
	• Do not speak while they are responding.	[ ]
	• Demonstrate appropriate body language and eye contact.	[ ]
	• Recognize any anger or negative emotions they may have.	[ ]
Plan & Support Change	• Thank your direct for letting you give them feedback.	[ ]
	• Answer any questions they may have about the feedback.	[ ]
	• Set a timeline for assessing changes in their behavior.	[ ]
	• Set clear goals with your direct so they act on the feedback.	[ ]
	• Ask your direct how you can support them with the feedback.	[ ]
Follow Up	• Ask your direct how the changes are going.	[ ]
	• Note any progress you observe based on the feedback.	[ ]
	• Use future 1:1s to follow up on progress.	[ ]
	• Remind directs about the feedback from time to time.	[ ]

Checklist for Effectively Receiving & Acting on Feedback in 1:1s

This tool serves as a reminder checklist for receiving and acting on feedback. Review each item and make a checkmark next to each—the more the better. Use unchecked items to improve how you receive and act on feedback in the future.

Feedback Stage	Key Behaviors	
Ask for Feedback	• Be specific when asking for what feedback you want.	[ ]
	• Communicate what you need clearly and concisely.	[ ]
	• Explain how you would like the feedback delivered ideally.	[ ]
	• Identify the goal(s) of receiving the feedback.	[ ]
	• Tell them what led to you wanting the feedback.	[ ]
Listen	• Actively listen to the feedback you are receiving.	[ ]
	• Do not respond until they are done talking.	[ ]
	• Be open-minded and curious about the feedback.	[ ]
	• Demonstrate appropriate body language and eye contact.	[ ]
	• Listen to understand rather than dispute the feedback.	[ ]
Think	• Absorb the feedback and what they had to say.	[ ]
	• Quell any anger or negative emotions you may have.	[ ]
	• Avoid becoming defensive when thinking about the feedback.	[ ]
	• Remind yourself the feedback is meant to help you.	[ ]

Feedback Stage	Key Behaviors	
Thank	• Thank them for giving you the feedback.	[ ]
	• Express gratitude even if you do not agree with the feedback.	[ ]
	• Build rapport by showing appreciation for their thoughts.	[ ]
Discuss	• Acknowledge you understand the feedback you just received.	[ ]
	• Clarify any questions you have about the feedback.	[ ]
	• Align with them on your perspectives of the feedback.	[ ]
	• Work together to create goals for acting on the feedback.	[ ]
	• Write down anything that will help you act on the feedback.	[ ]
	• Determine how progress will be assessed and a timeline.	[ ]
Change	• Use the feedback moving forward.	[ ]
	• Ask yourself daily how the feedback can be used.	[ ]
	• Create a spreadsheet to track your progress.	[ ]
	• Get an accountability partner to help you.	[ ]
	• Reflect on how you are progressing to address the feedback.	[ ]
Follow Up	• Follow up with the other person on challenges and obstacles.	[ ]
	• Let the other person know if you need any support.	[ ]
	• Discuss your progress in future 1:1s.	[ ]
	• As the timeline ends, reassess where you are at.	[ ]

SECTION 4
SPECIAL TOPICS

In this final section of the book, a few additional topics are covered. I start with skip-level 1:1s. Although much of what was discussed in this book applies, there is some additional nuance and issues to be aware of. I then discuss how to avoid the quagmire of too many meetings. Finally, all is tied together in the concluding chapter.

> *1:1s are all about building meaningful relationships with those you work with. They are arguably the most powerful mechanism to communicate richly and deeply, to provide two-way feedback, build trust and confidence, and align expectations. And, by doing so, you demonstrate that you are invested in your team members' success, and you foster emotional commitment.*
>
> Executive, TIAA

> *1:1s are a critical mechanism to engage with your team in a deep and meaningful way. This connection, in turn, helps foster alignment and most importantly, creates a sense of shared purpose and partnership.*
>
> Executive, JP Morgan Chase

14

Wait, There Are Skip-Level 1:1s?

If your actions inspire others to dream more, learn more, do more and become more, you are a leader.

John Quincy Adams

It is a terrible thing to look over your shoulder when you are trying to lead—and find no one there.

Franklin Roosevelt

Quotes from these former U.S. presidents set the stage for this chapter as they speak to the importance of leaders inspiring and connecting with others. One mechanism to do that is skip-level 1:1s—meetings between a team member and their manager's manager. Let me start with some data I recently collected. 55% of respondents indicated they do not have skip-level meetings, and 45% said they do. Meaning, skip-level 1:1s are clearly a work activity for many (nearly half) of employees. For those having them, there was a great deal of variability around how frequently they occur. The most typical cadence was once a quarter. Next I asked, are these skip-level 1:1s valuable to you? Here were their responses:

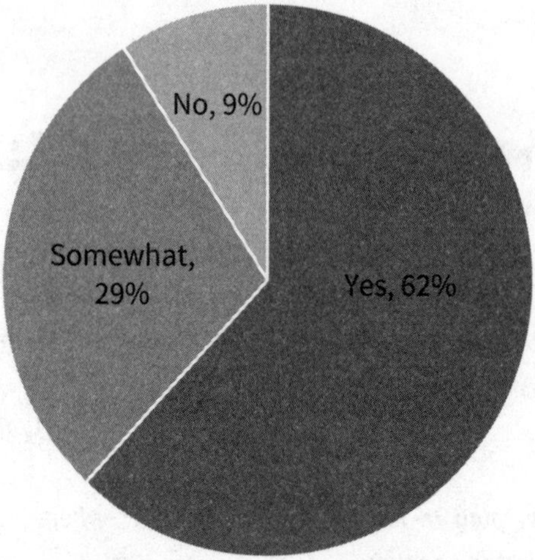

These results are quite striking. The fact that only 9% said "no" intrigued me. Clearly, respondents are seeing some value in the activity, despite most leaders never receiving formal training on the topic. Thus, I would contend, the potential of skip-level 1:1s is likely much higher. The final question I asked respondents was: "Do you wish you had skip-level 1:1s?" I asked this question to the entire data sample, those currently having them and those who did not. Most participants answered affirmatively to this question, with 57% reporting they wanted skip-level 1:1s. For those that said "no," three themes emerged:

1. **Doesn't Make Much Sense for Me**
   a. "My boss's boss is the chairman of the board so I would say 'no.'"
   b. "No, because my manager's manager is the CEO, and I don't expect that."
2. **Not Necessary to Have Formal Meetings/They Are Already Available**
   a. "We are pretty open around here, so if I want to talk to our director . . . I just ping him to talk."
   b. "Not really, as I can meet with her at will. Our VPs are very accessible."
3. **Doesn't Want to Work More Closely with the Skip-Level Leader**
   a. "Not really, she's a disorganized and awful communicator. I like her as a person, but I want to spend as little time with her as possible."
   b. "No. He's an interim and I don't particularly like him."

What was super interesting to me was that the reasons listed for not wanting skip-levels did not reflect a philosophical disagreement with the concept. They were more about the person in the skip-level role, job level of the direct, or not being necessary given other communication avenues in place. For those who said "yes," they *do* wish they had skip-level 1:1s, two interrelated themes emerged:

1. **Good for Alignment/Insight**
   a. "Yes – sometimes my work feels detached from the overall team's work. I think it would help integrate my work into what the team does and potentially improve my skill utilization."
   b. "It would be nice to get direct input on their priorities and feedback on my program areas from my manager's manager."
   c. "Yes. It would help us to understand each other better and better align."
   d. "Yes. I would love to hear from my manager's manager his strategic vision for our organization."
2. **Good for Relationship Building/Increase Visibility**
   a. "Yes. To get to know that manager better and give them a better understanding of my work."
   b. "Yes, to build that relationship."
   c. "Yes. Would give me the opportunity to be mentored by my supervisor's supervisor and learn directly about preferences for information and decision-making material needed for him/her and my supervisor. Would give me an opportunity to represent myself and create a direct relationship and not be an abstraction. Would allow me to learn what tools and tips have contributed most to their own success or what they see contributing most to the success of others as higher-level executives."
   d. "It would create more visibility for me throughout the organization."

The potential positives of skip-levels are certainly apparent in the quotes above. Stepping back, let's review the purposes of skip-level 1:1s.

The Goals of Skip-Level 1:1s

Skip-level meetings can serve a host of purposes. Below, I list those frequently mentioned by respondents:

- **Get a pulse on what's happening.** Skip-level managers are layers removed from the directs of their directs. Skip-levels are a way for these employees to share feedback on their projects, teams, and overall organization. As one interviewee suggested, using a military analogy, you can get "on-the-ground" truth by meeting with your directs' directs. Skip-levels are also a great mechanism to get a sense of how your own directs are doing as managers. Note, this is not meant in any way to "spy" on a manager. As is discussed throughout this chapter, we don't want to undermine the manager by using skip-levels. With that said, skip-levels can help ameliorate the common concern that employees often leave bad managers. Skip-level 1:1s can tackle that head-on and in a constructive way. These meetings create the opportunity for directs to talk about any morale or management issues to a manager more removed than their immediate manager. And, getting this feedback on your direct, from their direct, is a great way for you to learn how to help your direct improve as a manager and avoid costly turnover.
- **Build trust.** It's important to develop and invest in relationships with those at different levels in your organization. Establishing skip-level relationships will help more junior team members stay engaged and attached to the organization. If you work to build rapport with lower-level employees, they'll be more likely to come to you when they have ideas or when they are struggling and feel like they have nowhere else to go. Skip-level meetings make you more human and approachable.
- **Get feedback on ideas.** Skip-level directs are at a valuable vantage point to evaluate and comment on ideas and initiatives you are pondering. For example, say you are considering the creation of a new incentive plan to promote higher levels of internal and external service quality. Gathering feedback from your

skip-level directs helps you determine if the plan is a good fit for all levels of the organization and will be received as intended.

- **Share information and counsel.** A skip-level 1:1 provides a space for you to share information in a more personal way. This can be information about a specific project, the team, or the organization. It also can be used for counsel on career development or discussing future goals and milestones. Hearing directly from you as their manager's manager can be incredibly helpful for more deeply embracing and accepting the information and counsel.

Overall, skip-levels give you an opportunity to gather and share information, make meaningful connections, and really dive in to see what is happening in your team and with your own directs. Also, scheduling skip-levels communicates that people—at all levels in the organization—are valuable and worth your time. Further, if you combine all of the information you hear across these employees, you may see patterns that can be very helpful to the execution of your role.

Implementing Skip-Level Meetings

There are 8 implementation steps for skip-level 1:1s (a checklist of best practices for skip-levels are included in the tools section). There are certainly parallels with 1:1s between a manager and their directs, but differences do exist.

Step 1: Inform Your Own Directs

If your manager were to start scheduling skip-level meetings with your directs without telling you, you'd probably be quite concerned and taken aback. Just like you wouldn't want your manager to do this, **don't simply start having skip-level 1:1s with your directs' directs.** First, you need to be sure to explain to your immediate directs why you're starting skip-levels and address any of their initial concerns. It's important how you frame this effort. Here is some potential language to consider for an email or at a larger meeting:

New Initiative

gordon@company.com

New Initiative

Gordon,

I want to tell you about a new employee engagement and experience initiative I will be starting. I will be scheduling occasional skip-level 1:1 meetings with your direct reports to get a read on strategy, develop relationships with them, and gain a greater understanding of their perspectives and experiences in their roles.

My overall intention with these skip levels is to do my part in helping our broader function and those within it thrive and grow. I will also be sure to share any common feedback or comments that are relative to you as their manager. I want to be clear, I am not undermining your leadership or second guessing your managerial skills. I am starting this practice with all of my directs with the goal of getting a pulse on the organization, our teams, and the employees that comprise them. Do let me know if you have or hear any feedback from your team members on the value of these skip-levels and/or ideas for improvement.

Best,
Sasha
The Manager

If you set clear expectations and have a trusting relationship with your directs, they will more readily buy into the practice of skip-levels and not feel threatened. After doing a few rounds of skip-levels, check back in with your directs to gauge how this is working from their perspective. This will make sure they feel valued, included, and an active part of the process.

Step 2: Inform Your Skip-Level Team Members

If you don't have a previously established relationship or regular contact with your skip-level directs, they may be confused about you requesting to meet with them 1:1. They could jump to the conclusion that something is wrong. To avoid this, communicate your intentions and expectations in advance. Make sure they know they are not in trouble, and this is not intended to check in (i.e., spy) on them or their manager. Here is a sample communication you can have, again via email or as part of a conversation/meeting:

> *I will be starting a new practice with you and your team members, where I schedule occasional 1:1 meetings for us—called skip-level 1:1s. This will be a time where we can get to know each other, talk about what is going well and not so well, and share feedback and information with one another. I will come prepped with a few questions for you, but if there is anything you want to discuss we can start there. Ideas for improving the team, anything you think I should know about, and other content like that is very welcome. I am also happy to chat about career issues more broadly. Our first skip-level meeting will be <DATE & TIME>. Let me know if this works for you. I look forward to it!"*

When you make your intentions and expectations for these meetings clear from the start, it mitigates the risk of people having the wrong idea or jumping to inaccurate conclusions.

Step 3: Create Your Skip-Level Schedule

Pick a 1:1 frequency that allows you to connect with all your skip-level directs but does not overly tax you. A rotation strategy is most common. These skip-levels could be quarterly or potentially monthly, depending on team sizes. Typically, these meetings are 20 or 30 minutes in length. The key is for you to do a small number each week, but not too many where you feel overwhelmed.

> *If your span of control is very large (e.g., more than 50 people), you can hold skip-level meeting in groups to maintain efficiency. While this strategy certainly saves time, it is much more difficult to foster personal connections and relationships in a group context. It may also affect the entire information-gathering process, given group dynamics, conformity pressures, and the like.*

I do want to stress that if your span of control is not large, that does not mean you should have weekly or biweekly skip-levels. An overly frequent skip-level cadence can become problematic, as it can undermine the manager. Avoid this. While skip-level meetings are a great practice, your primary communication and point of contact should be with your own directs.

Step 4: Build the Agenda

Agendas for skip-levels are a bit different from typical 1:1s discussed so far. It is often the case that the skip-level direct may not have any pressing questions or requests for help or support from you as their skip-level manager. Thus, start with giving the team member space to ask any questions on their mind, but then move to asking a set of general questions.

Some examples of questions to ask are:

- How are things going for you?
- Anything on your mind that I may be able to help with or just talk about?
- What am I not seeing that would be helpful for me to know?
- From your perspective, how is the team doing and how is team morale?
- What obstacles are you facing in your role?
- Do you feel you understand how your work fits with the organization's goals?
- What would make work better for you?
- Do you feel supported with your career progress and goals?
- If you oversaw the team, what is one thing you would do differently?
- Is there anything that we did not cover that you would like to discuss?

You would pick the questions that feel appropriate and right for your relationship with your skip-level direct. If they wish to talk about their immediate manager, **here are some follow-up questions:**

- What's the best part of working with your manager?
- What's the most challenging part of working with your manager?
- What do you wish your manager would do more or less often?
- What is a recent situation you wish your manager handled differently?
- What is a recent situation that you think your manager handled well?
- How often do you have conversations with your manager about your career? How do these conversations typically go?

The goal with these questions is not for you to report everything or even anything you hear back to the manager. You are generally focused on uncovering themes across skip-level directs that appear important. Even if themes are uncovered, however, it does not mean you would share with your direct. It all depends on what you are learning. With this said, there may be issues with some key or high potential talent that is not part of a theme but could warrant a conversation with the manager to avoid turnover. Whatever you do based on what you learn, be highly sensitive to inadvertently creating a scenario where the skip-level direct experiences retribution from their manager due to talking to you.

Step 5: Develop Rapport

Rapport building is critical in skip-levels, especially given that meeting with their manager's manager can engender anxiety due to the power differential. Finding commonalities with your skip-level directs makes conversations and connections easier. See what you can find out about your skip-level team members from your direct (their manager) in advance to help pave the way. For example, do you share common interests with them? Share the same hometown? Hobbies? Have kids the same age? It is important that you demonstrate that you want to get to know them as individuals. Building this connection is key, especially in the initial meetings. Review Chapter 6 to see potential questions designed for getting to know one another better.

Step 6: Interact Effectively

Chapters 8 through 10 discuss the facilitation process in 1:1s, including critical skills such as listening with empathy. All that content surely matters in skip-level 1:1s, but what I want to focus on here is the statement: *"Have you talked to your manager about this?"* There will be certain situations that are brought to your attention during skip-levels that their direct manager is better equipped to deal with. That's why it's critical to ask your skip-level team member if they have brought the issue to their immediate manager. Their answer will reveal valuable insights. For example, maybe they hadn't thought to approach their manager about it, or maybe they were afraid to. Perhaps their manager took surprising action or came up with a solution to the issue without asking for their direct's input first. You certainly want your skip-level team members to know they can come to you with these challenges, but you also need to emphasize that their manager should be their first point of contact. If they're not, it's important to understand why and then address it. You can then coach their manager on how to develop trust and build their own rapport with their directs to open these communication lines.

Step 7: Praise Your Skip-Level Directs

Praise costs you nothing but can have such a positive impact on those receiving it. If you hear someone is excelling in their job—tell them! Genuine and specific praise from a leader higher up in the organization will likely feel like a tremendous gift. Ask your directs about which skip-level team members are stars, who's going above and beyond, and who has high potential. Make praise a part of your skip-level 1:1s to demonstrate that the organization values and appreciates the work of its people.

Step 8: Follow Up and Follow Through

If relevant, make it clear what you will do following the meeting, whether it is addressing problems, sharing information, or implementing their feedback and suggestions. This will help build trust and give your skip-level members confidence in coming to you again. Make sure the team member is clear on their actions as well—whether it involves sending you information, doing their part to address an issue, or acting on your advice. It is important that you both are owning part of the takeaways from these conversations.

Avoid The Big Problem

I want to circle back to a key theme I have been trying to emphasize in this chapter: **Be careful not to undermine your directs (the managers of your skip-level directs).** Given your leadership level, the simplest "that sounds good" could be heard by the skip-level direct as "great idea, let's do it!" Namely, top bosses' suggestions are often experienced as orders. Thus, you need to be highly sensitive to the words you use. Your goal is to learn, not to communicate agreement or disagreement. You are not replacing your direct as your skip-level directs' manager. You should always consult and communicate with their manager as needed, especially around themes you are observing across your skip-levels.

Following all these implementation steps might feel like a large investment—one you may feel you don't have time for. However, I would argue that the benefits of skip-level 1:1s warrant the time needed to have them, especially given the potential positive impact that skip-level meetings can have on you and your directs' effectiveness as leaders, employee engagement and connection, and the culture of the broader team. Let me conclude with a quote from an interview with an executive at TIAA:

> *Skip-levels give you an incredible wealth of information. They give you an opportunity to really dive in and see what is really happening, to validate what you are hearing, make connections, and see what is what. Also, skip-levels communicate that all are valuable and you are approachable.*

Key Takeaways

- **Skip-levels Are Helpful.** Skip-level 1:1s are meetings between you and your directs' directs. While these meetings aren't meant for you to take over as their manager, skip-levels are a great way for you to gain insight "on the ground" and to provide higher-up support to the team. Skip-levels are similar to the 1:1s you have with your directs but serve a different purpose. These 1:1s are used to get a pulse on what's happening in your team and those you oversee, build trust between different levels of the team, and share information and counsel. They aren't as frequently held but can provide insight that your regular 1:1s might not fully reveal.
- **Don't Just Start Having Skip-Levels.** I repeat, *do not just start having skip-levels*. Your first step in setting these meetings up for success is to let your immediate directs know that you plan to have them and why. Field any questions or concerns they may have, reiterating the true purpose of these meetings. Then do the same with your skip-level directs. If you fail to do these steps, your skip-level 1:1s may be experienced like micromanaging, or may give the impression that there is a problem with their manager, or that the team is in trouble.

- **Set Skip-Levels Up for Success.** After discussing why these meetings will be happening, create a schedule for doing them. Furthermore, make sure you set up agendas and focus on developing rapport, especially early on. Hear what your skip-level direct would like to talk about and go from there, but have your standard questions ready to go. End the meetings by praising skip-level directs where you can and follow up on any action items you have committed to accomplishing.
- **Don't Undermine Your Own Directs.** Skip-levels are a great way to get insight about your directs as managers, but don't undermine them. For example, don't agree with ideas your skip-level direct has, as this ultimately falls on your own directs and they may have their own input on the ideas. Instead, listen with an open mind and ask if your skip-level direct has talked to their manager about the idea. Also, use their concerns and issues to support and develop your own directs' leadership skills.

15

I Am Drowning in Meetings. What Do I Do?

Meeting activity is incredibly high for most all professionals, and the thought of adding more meetings to your calendar might seem ludicrous. To help make some room, strategies to decrease wasted and unproductive meeting time are shared, especially as it relates to meetings you directly lead or that occur within the function/team you lead. This chapter is not strictly about 1:1 meetings. It is about all your other meetings. It is about streamlining and improving your time in meeting activity more broadly so that the addition of 1:1s with your team members feels easier and a lighter lift to do.

Strategies to Decrease Wasted Time in Meetings

As a leader, your role in changing meeting culture and practices is central. However, meetings are inherently a shared experience—they are a social phenomenon. Given this, the collective must be actively involved in the process of change. New conversations with your team are needed. Conversations where fresh understandings and paths are forged. Conversations designed to break rhythms and start new, healthier routines. I want to outline two conversations I suggest having with your teams to better manage your meeting load.

Conversation 1: When to Meet or Not to Meet

This conversation is about getting everyone aligned with when a meeting is even needed in general. Namely, before hitting send on a meeting invite, ask yourself three questions: 1) Is there a compelling purpose to meet? 2) Does that purpose necessitate people to interact/engage with the content to assure success and foster buy-in? 3) Are there other communication tools that could be more efficient for the purpose (an asynchronous meeting, an email, etc.)? If the answers are, Yes, Yes, and No, a meeting is warranted. To help the team best understand these guidelines, walk through different common meeting scenarios. For each scenario, collectively decide whether a meeting would be needed or whether a different communication vehicle—and which one(s)—would be a better fit. Get collective agreement on this to amplify new norms and expectations.

Next, do a meeting audit with the team. Review all reoccurring meetings. For each, see if it can be eliminated, reduced in time, or reduced in frequency. Next, for each recurring meeting, decide on who should attend regularly, who should attend periodically, who should attend for just part of the meeting (e.g., they are relevant for just one part of the agenda), and who should just be kept in the loop, such as by sending them the minutes afterwards. The above exercises could even be done anonymously through a quick survey if you are worried that team members won't be forthcoming.

Using feedback from the audit should allow you to significantly reduce your and your team's overall meeting load. However, I do want to add that there is often a much bigger issue here when it comes to meeting load. My research shows that leaders and organizations that prioritize everything as being important have way more meetings than leaders and organizations that are more careful and strategic with their prioritization. If you carefully select and manage your key priorities, you will still have to make choices meeting-by-meeting on whether you need to meet. However, you are getting the meeting load issue under control more broadly. Remember, reducing meetings without reducing priorities can have unintended consequences, as meetings are still central to employee involvement, building relationships, and inclusion. Given this, while I am a fan of a meeting reduction diet that is principled, my preference is to make meetings more effective, shorter, and leaner as mechanisms to give time back—which leads to the next conversation.

Conversation 2: Cutting Meeting Times

Talk to the team about being intentional and thoughtful around how long meetings should be and not just using the default settings (e.g., 60-minute block) on your local calendar software/app. As before, different types of actual and hypothetical meetings can be discussed to calibrate collective expectations. The hope is that a host of meetings can be made shorter through this process. This is particularly important given something called Parkinson Law—the idea that work expands to fill whatever time is allotted to it.[1] So, if a meeting is scheduled for one hour, magically it will take . . . one hour. The same goes for a meeting scheduled for 30 minutes. But, we can use this to our advantage. Don't hesitate to schedule your meetings for non-traditional durations like 20 or 25 minutes instead of 30 minutes or 45 or 50 minutes instead of 60 minutes. The meeting will more than likely still accomplish what it was intended to, because dialing the meeting time back also creates positive pressure. Research shows that groups operating under some level of pressure perform more optimally given increased focus and urgency.[2] Therefore, shortening meetings won't just save you time, but may also result in better, more efficient outcomes. As a leader, experiment with your meeting times. Cut them back. Look for opportunities to give time back—this is the gift that we are all craving. Take the challenge. Reduce meeting times and then reflect as a team on how it is all working.

Both conversations help pave the way for a new future of work from a collaboration perspective. They should help return time to all. There is another piece to this puzzle, however. Make meeting time more effective. If your meetings are more effective, you likely won't need as many, because the meetings you do have will produce more clear and compelling outcomes.

Better Meetings

I have interviewed thousands of meeting attendees around the globe about meeting leadership. The best meeting leaders appear to have something in common—they share a similar mindset where they recognize their role as a steward of others' time. Interestingly, leaders often adopt a stewardship mindset when the meeting is with key customers or key bosses because they would never want these individuals to leave the meeting saying, "that was a waste of time." However, stewardship is often disregarded when meeting with one's team and/or peers—we tend to be a bit lazy with our meeting choices and facilitation when we see meetings as being lower in stakes. This is highly problematic as time is valuable to all, not just those who are higher in an organization or those we need something from. When you adopt a stewardship mindset, you become intentional with your meeting decisions and approaches from start to finish. Preparing for effectiveness is not an afterthought. And being intentional and making smart meeting choices does not take much time at all—it can take a minute of time with practice. But it does take some forethought. To help with this issue, let me outline some choices to be made, broken down by pre-meeting practices, during-the-meeting practices, and end-of-meeting practices.

Pre-Meeting Practices

Compelling agendas. Tailor agendas to set the stage for effectiveness. We all know the basics of agendas (e.g., gather input from attendees on it, distribute in advance), so I will jump to an innovation in agendas that can promote inclusion and effectiveness. As opposed to a set of topics to be discussed, try organizing the agenda as a set of questions to be answered. This action causes the meeting leader to really think about the meeting and what they are hoping to achieve. By framing agenda items as questions, you have a better sense of who really must be invited to the meeting, as they are relevant to the questions. By framing agenda items as questions, you know when to end the meeting and if the meeting has been successful—when and if the questions have been answered. By framing agenda items as questions, you create an engaging challenge for attendees that draws them in. And if you just can't think of any questions, it likely means you don't need a meeting.

Actively manage meeting size. Larger meetings, even with the best of intentions, undermine inclusion as there is less airtime for attendees, greater coordination issues, and even something called social loafing—where we don't engage as deeply during interactions with others because we feel more anonymous in larger groups, akin to hiding in a crowd.[3] Therefore, the larger the meeting, the more likely attendees are to socially loaf. Plus, larger meetings are associated with poorer evaluations of meeting quality.[4] So, don't over-invite. You may want to invite everyone so they feel included, but that is a false solution to inclusion. However—and this is a big however—our research shows that while employees often complain about meetings, they also get worried if they are not invited to meetings. Accordingly, to avoid team members feeling marginalized if they are not invited, a conversation or email is needed in advance. This is all tied to the fear of missing out (FOMO). There are three parts to these conversations to help lessen FOMO:

1. Give a good explanation as to why their attendance is not needed, as this makes the lack of an invitation not feel personal.

2. Give them the opportunity to provide input in advance on any of the topics that will be discussed in the meeting, which will help them still feel valued

3. Commit to good notetaking around key takeaways and action items and then send these notes to them after the meeting, which will address their potential anxiety of missing the meeting.

Finally, one pre-meeting practice that can help for reducing meeting sizes is to consider inviting people for part of the meeting, but not all the meeting. Leverage the agenda to time entry and exit of these attendees. This lets you be more inclusive and effective, without the bloat. You'll also save these attendees time, which they will appreciate.

Use video in virtual meetings (if possible). We need to create presence, as it promotes engagement and inclusion. Video increases the chances of that happening and serves to decrease multitasking. Yes, it can increase fatigue, but I would rather handle meeting fatigue differently—namely by shrinking meeting sizes, shrinking meeting times, and making meetings more effective. These are the bigger determinants of meeting fatigue that I have found. As an aside, another good way to handle fatigue is to build meeting-free breaks into your calendar and be sure to stretch and move around between meetings. Finally, turn off self-view in the virtual meeting itself. In this option, your camera is still on and others can see you, but you can't see yourself. Hiding self-view is so simple but so useful, as looking at ourselves, which is what we tend to do during self-view, is a key reason we experience mental drain and "zoom fatigue" as it is unnatural and triggers excessive self-evaluation.[5]

During-the-Meeting Practices

Start the meeting well, as it sets the stage for effectiveness, engagement, and inclusion. As the meeting leader, your mood matters. Research suggests it produces a contagion effect on attendees—where attendees' mood mirrors yours.[6] Start the meeting with energy, appreciation, and gratitude, especially during challenging times. Doing so increases the chances of a more positive meeting mood state, which matters as it promotes more participation, creativity, listening, and constructiveness—all essential to meeting inclusion and effectiveness.[7] I am not at all suggesting leaders should be artificially positive, but even in difficult circumstances we can display energy, appreciation, and most certainly can display gratitude.

Active facilitation. Meeting leaders must embrace the role of facilitator. Draw attendees in (e.g., "Sandy, please share your thoughts") to keep them engaged and included. Avoid generically asking, "Any comments?" Also, don't let an attendee ramble and go off topic; kindly interrupt if necessary so others can engage. That is your job as a meeting leader, and all attendees are hoping you will do this. Also, encourage attendees of larger virtual meetings to use chat. My initial research on chat suggests it is a key mechanism to bringing more voices into the conversation. Assign someone to monitor the chat if too much is on your plate as a meeting leader.

Diversify how you run your meetings. Mix it up. Diversification of approaches to meetings serves to energize and engage attendees. For example, try using silence in your meetings, at times. Silence can promote effectiveness and inclusion like almost no other. Research supports the benefits of silence in meetings as a way of gathering more ideas, perspectives, and insights from attendees. For example, if you compare groups brainstorming in silence (e.g., typing directly into a document) versus those brainstorming with their mouths, silent brainstorming groups yield nearly twice as many ideas, and those ideas tend to be even more creative.[8] Why would silent brainstorming result in more and better ideas? When communicating via writing, all can "talk" at once. There is no waiting for your turn. Additionally, there is less filtering of ideas given the simultaneous generation of ideas. Here is the good news: silence can be done very easily in a meeting by just sharing a Google Doc with attendees during the actual meeting (there are many purveyors of virtual whiteboard apps that could be used as well). This document should contain key questions that need to be answered or prompts for brainstorming. All attendees are encouraged to contribute to the document for, say, 15 minutes or whatever makes sense for the task at hand. During this window, attendees should be actively generating ideas, commenting on others' input, and collaborating actively via writing. Once the time is up, the leader can debrief and identify themes, conclusions, and next steps. Or if outcomes are not fully apparent, the meeting can end for now and you can circle back with attendees once you reflect on the document. By the way, even meetings focused on providing updates lend themselves to this technique. Each person can just type their update into a shared document, and attendees can then review and comment. This is extremely efficient and can even be done asynchronously, which is a bonus. Give it a try.

End of the Meetings

Don't run over. While starting meetings late seems to cause stress, our research shows that ending meetings late is a greater source of stress for many, so end meetings well. ***Meetings must have a defined ending period.*** With a few minutes left, be sure to clarify takeaways. For each takeaway, identify the DRIs, or directly responsible individuals. During the close, key notes can be recorded. The point is not to capture a full play-by-play of the meeting, but rather to provide a concise synopsis of the key points and action items in a format that makes the information as accessible as possible for both those who attended the meeting, and maybe even more importantly, those who did not attend. By the way, if you use the questions approach to agendas, you can record answers as notes and share with attendees and non-attendees.

For meetings you don't control (others are calling and leading them), your options for decreasing time in poor meetings are limited. One strategy that can provide some help is to schedule meetings differently, if possible. Namely, block off time on your calendar for uninterrupted deep work. Try hard to hold that time sacred. Then, allow your meetings to be scheduled outside that block of time. Next, do a review of your regularly occurring meetings. Are there meetings that you don't really need to be at or are just not a good use of your time? For those meeting that are not critical, consider approaching the leader about attending part of the meeting (where it is relevant to you), but not all of the meeting. Alternatively, you can have a conversation with the leader about not attending all the meetings. Instead, you can attend one out of every three or four. For the others, you can just stay in the loop through the reading of meeting minutes. Of course, you can also give the leader the option of indicating any of these meetings that they think you really need to go to. Finally, for any new meetings that come up, if you just don't think you are needed, reach out to the leader to have a conversation around this and see where it goes. Typically, meeting leaders realize they are over-inviting in the name of inclusion. When checked, they are usually very happy to pare the invite list down.

Broader Organizational Strategies to Decrease the Number of Meetings

Organizations have tried many different strategies to decrease meeting time and to improve meetings. I will outline a small set that have worked well for some organizations that I've worked with. Not all these practices will make sense for your organization. But, some just might. I recognize that you personally might not be positioned to implement these strategies. I still wanted to include them to provide a complete picture of meeting improvement options.

1. Some organizations require approval from more senior manager for large meetings (e.g., over 10 people). This might sound a bit draconian, but it does result in more careful thought when making the meeting invite list, which is key.
2. Assign a member of the senior leadership team ownership of meetings as a key work process. By doing so, the monitoring, attention, and improvement of meetings becomes part of the organizational fabric. We do this for other extremely expensive work processes and activities. For example, we want our technology investment to be overseen by the Chief Technology or information officer.
3. Change calendar systems to default to reduced meeting times (e.g., 25 minutes and 50 minutes).
4. Assess meeting effectiveness on engagement and pulse surveys. Create a meeting metrics dashboard and tie these to financial indicators so meetings can be costed out readily. This all serves to create accountability for making meetings better.

5. Build meeting leadership skill development into talent systems such as onboarding, high-potential initiatives, coaching, and training.
6. Consider the use of meeting-free time periods. The data are quite mixed on whether this approach works, but it still has potential if implemented effectively.

Conclusion

All of the above suggestions should help return time back to your team, but most importantly it should serve to make the time in meetings more effective. While you can't control other's meetings, you can control your own. You can make excellent meeting choices. You can demonstrate stewardship. You can be the example that you hope others will follow in promoting meeting effectiveness. Each meeting is your opportunity to do your part on promoting effectiveness and address the meeting overload issue. Take the challenge. Take the challenge so that you can more readily find time to implement and carry out your 1:1s with excellence to maximize gains.

Key Takeaways

- **Eliminating Meetings Is Not the Solution.** While employees often complain about the number of meetings they have, meetings are still an essential piece of organizational democracy. However, there are strategies to reduce the number and increase the effectiveness of meetings to combat the negative effects of too many meetings.
- **Have a Conversation with Your Team.** As a leader, you control your meetings. Start by having two conversations about your meetings. First, set expectations around when meetings are warranted and when they are not. Use these new norms to audit your current recurring meetings and adjust accordingly. Second, talk about cutting back the time meetings are held for,

such as by holding what has been a 60-minute meeting for 50 minutes. Having these conversations will reduce the number and time spent in meetings, which your team will thank you for.

- **Increase Meeting Effectiveness.** Rather than eliminating meetings, the goal is to make meetings more effective, which will save rework time and allay fatigue and frustration. There are various tactics you can use as a leader that can help with this, which can be broken down into pre-meeting, during-the-meeting, and end-of-meeting practices. Examples of such practices include creating compelling agendas, actively facilitating the meetings to boost energy, experimenting with different strategies such as silent brainstorming, and having a proper close to a meeting to assure action.
- **Organizational Strategies Exist.** I have found a variety of tactics organizations themselves use to reduce the overall number of meetings they have. These range from requiring approval for larger meetings to including meeting metrics on engagement surveys. While these may be harder for you to influence and these tactics vary by organization, they do help in the pursuit of lowering the number of overall meetings.

16

Final Thoughts—It's About Values

It isn't what we say or think that defines us, but what we do.
Jane Austen, author of *Pride and Prejudice* and *Sense and Sensibility*

This quote resonates with me. Our behaviors define us. Our behaviors signal what is important to us and what our values truly are. I often ask leaders about their aspirational values—what they hope to do and be known for. I get many different responses, but there are some responses that are very common across people. Values such as:

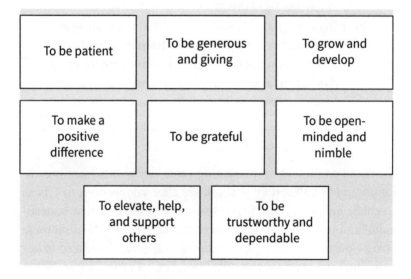

To be patient	To be generous and giving	To grow and develop
To make a positive difference	To be grateful	To be open-minded and nimble
To elevate, help, and support others	To be trustworthy and dependable	

Each of these values has a meaningful connection to 1:1s. Namely, 1:1s serve as a key mechanism for embodying these values and most importantly, living your values.

1:1s are also fundamental to organizational values. Let me illustrate by sharing some value statements from well-known organizations. In each, I bold the values clearly aligned with effective 1:1s.

Intel	Customer First, Fearless Innovation, Results Driven, **One Intel, Inclusion, Quality, and Integrity—guide how we make decisions, treat each other,** serve our customers to achieve their goals, and shape technology as a force for good. We are **united by our purpose** and **driven by our values** to achieve our ambitions and help our customers succeed.
IBM	Dedication to every client's success; Innovation that matters, for our company and for the world; **Trust and personal responsibility in all relationships.**
TIAA	Put the client first; We inspire confidence; **Value our people; We take care of each other**; Act with integrity; **We do the right thing.**
Adobe	Genuine; Exceptional (**committed to creating exceptional experiences that delight our employees** and customers); Innovative; **Involved (we're inclusive, open, and actively engaged with our** customers, partners, **employees,** and the communities we serve).

I could go on and on presenting value statements from organizations, and in almost all you will see clear connections to 1:1s as a vehicle for expressing these values. How ideal is it that a meaningful and positively impactful activity like 1:1s can check all these boxes—personal values, organizational values, and be related to key individual and team success outcomes. Yes, 1:1s are a choice. But in many ways, I would argue that 1:1s are an obligation—they are the embodiment of leadership and a core way of expressing values at all levels.

Are there companies with policies around 1:1s, such as how they should be conducted and how often? In my interviews with top leaders across a wide range of sectors, with the exception of Cisco, I found no organizations with any formal policies around how to conduct 1:1s other than those around performance management. Instead, each manager is left to navigate this process on their own. 1:1s might be quite normative in some companies or for some leaders. But, rarely do companies have any formal, universal guidelines or system on how to effectively conduct them or an explicit requirement to do them. To help promote this, a process for creating an organization-wide system for 1:1s can be found in the tools shared at the end of this book section.

Conclusion

1:1s are a critical investment in your people. Do they take a lot of time? Absolutely. But in some regards, not really. For example, meeting 30 minutes each week or 60 minutes every other week with one of your team members totals to around 25 hours over the course of a year. Is that too much time to meet with your team members given the incredible outcomes associated with well-executed 1:1s? The answer is "no" based on the science showing how weekly and biweekly 1:1s promote key outcomes like engagement, performance, and retention. The answer is "no" if you embrace the notion that 1:1s allow you to express your aspirational values. The answer is "no" if the well-being and success of your people is important to you.

I do want to emphasize, while the focus of this book has been on 1:1s between managers and directs, so much of what was discussed is relevant to other types of 1:1s—be it 1:1s with peers, customers, or vendors. Helping others feel seen and heard transcends all relationships. Addressing both personal and practical needs of others transcends all relationships. Developing trust and acting on commitments transcends all relationships. I will conclude this book with a Buddhist quote, "*The value of life is not based on how long we live, but how much we contribute to others in our society.*" 1:1s allow us to contribute deeply and meaningfully to people, to teams, and to our organizations. And by doing so, we can look in the mirror knowing that we are doing our small part in lifting others and elevating the human condition as it relates to work.

Key Takeaways

- **1:1s Embody Your Values.** Our behaviors signal our values, and our values tell others what is important to us. 1:1s are a critical way for you to support your people, demonstrate your leadership abilities, and improve key outcomes for your team and organization. Therefore, while 1:1s may be seen as a choice, I would argue they are an obligation. I hope this book convinces you of that and is helpful in the journey ahead in establishing your own effective 1:1s.

Section 4 Tools

Two tools are shared here:

1. Checklist of Best Practices for Skip-Level 1:1s
2. Creating an Organization-Wide System for 1:1s—A Suggested Process

Checklist of Best Practices for Skip-Level 1:1s

This tool is a checklist for introducing and/or evaluating your current skip-level 1:1 practices.

Step	Description	Used?
Inform Your Own Directs	Before doing anything else, you **must** inform your own directs about the meetings. Explain their purpose, specifically with what these meetings are (and are not), and answer any of their questions. If you fail to do this step, skip-levels can undermine your relationships with your directs and erode trust.	[ ]
Inform Your Skip-Level Directs	Next, have the same conversation in step 1 with your skip-level directs. Make sure to explain that these meetings are not being held because they are in trouble, but are rather meant to give them face time with you and develop your relationship together.	[ ]
Create Your Skip-Level Schedule	After establishing expectations, create your skip-level schedule. These meetings are not as frequently held as regular 1:1s, but should be done with all skip-level directs. Make sure the schedule does not overtax you in any particular week.	[ ]
Build the Agenda	Agendas for skip-levels are a bit different than regular 1:1s. Come prepared with some general questions to get them speaking. Assess what they're comfortable talking about and see what you both can learn. Provide room for them to ask questions on their minds.	[ ]

Step	Description	Used?
Develop Rapport	There are two levels between you and your skip-level direct, which can be intimidating for them. Be cognizant of this power difference. Work hard to make a connection. Find commonalities with them to reduce anxiety. Doing so will lead to more open and honest conversations.	[ ]
Interact Effectively	Ask questions. Listen carefully. Show empathy. Share information and perspectives. Engage with what is on their minds. Be as forthcoming as you can. The key here is to **never overstep your own direct report (their manager)**. Always ask if your skip-level direct asked their own manager first and be careful of agreeing to actions until consulting with their manager.	[ ]
Praise Your Skip-Level Directs	Praising skip-level directs costs you nothing but can mean the world to them. Make sure to recognize their great work when warranted. To aid in this, ask your own directs about what to commend and celebrate across their people.	[ ]
Follow Up and Follow Through	Make sure to follow up after the meeting on anything requiring follow-up. Encourage the skip-level direct to follow-up with their manager as well, if necessary. And, if you promised to do something such as sending information, make sure to do so.	[ ]

Creating an Organization-Wide System for 1:1s—A Suggested Process

The checklist below walks you through steps for creating an organization-wide system for 1:1s. The approach is inspired from research on the successful implementation of HR and change management initiatives along with insights gleaned from Cisco's innovative approach to company-wide 1:1s. This process can be adapted based on your organization's history with change, culture, and needs.

Check	Steps
[ ]	**IDENTIFY CHAMPION(S).** Identify champion(s) from senior leadership (e.g., CHRO, COO, Division President) who will be the "face" of the system.
[ ]	**ASSEMBLE TEAM.** Assemble a cross-divisional implementation team to flesh out the program and to ensure that the created system fits well with different functions and job levels.
[ ]	**ESTABLISH VISION.** Document the key hopes, goals, targets, and overall operating principles for the 1:1 system. When doing so, be sure to connect the 1:1 approach to organizational values and other HR/talent systems to promote integration and mitigate "flavor of the month" perceptions that new initiatives can often engender. The goals identified here will also serve as the evaluation criteria in a subsequent step.

Check	Steps
[ ]	**CREATE SYSTEM DETAILS.** Leverage the learnings from this book to decide on how structured the system should be for leaders, such as having required cadences and templates versus allowing the leader to tailor to their desires. Relatedly, decide on how technology will or won't be used to facilitate the 1:1 system. An informal approach simply leveraging shared online or paper templates and documents can be used, or a more formal system can be used where technology serves to structure the process involving team member input, leader review, and action planning. A great example of a formal system can be found on the Cisco website: https://www.cisco.com/c/r/team-development/teamspace/checkins.html
[ ]	**COMMUNICATE THROUGH MULTIPLE CHANNELS.** Communicate actively and transparently to all the "hows" and "whys" of the 1:1 initiative. Address common concerns of starting 1:1s via the system (e.g., a detailed FAQ). At the same time, prepare individual leaders to discuss the initiative with their teams and answer questions themselves.
[ ]	**PROVIDE TRAINING.** Provide comprehensive training to assure an understanding of 1:1s and the process, vision, implementation, and broader expectations of the 1:1 system.
[ ]	**LAUNCH AND SUPPORT THE SYSTEM.** Create a meaningful launch event to generate excitement. Once the system is launched and live, provide coaching and support to leaders and team members to be sure questions and problems are addressed.

Check	Steps
[ ]	**MONITOR PROGRESS.** If you created a more formal technology-driven system, monitor use of the system via a dashboard. If you decide on a more informal system, assess use and evaluation of the system via pulse surveys or integrating survey questions into the current engagement survey system.
[ ]	**EVALUATE AND ASSSESS IMPACT.** Evaluate the impact of the system on key outcomes of importance to the organization. For example, is the intended use of the system correlated with employee engagement and retention? The key criteria evaluated should be those identified in the vision statement for the system. Ideally, try to collect evaluation data such that leaders can get some feedback on how to do 1:1s most effectively.
[ ]	**UPDATE SYSTEM.** Based on team member and leader evaluation and comments, tweak and alter the 1:1 system as needed to maximize its value. Evaluate any changes so that the system can keep being improved over time.

Notes

Preface: Vision, Approach, and the Science

1. https://blog.lucidmeetings.com/blog/how-many-meetings-are-there-per-day-in-2022
2. van Eerde, W., & Buengeler, C. (2015). Meetings all over the world: Structural and psychological characteristics of meetings in different countries. In J. A. Allen, N. Lehmann-Willenbrock, & S. G. Rogelberg (Eds.), *The Cambridge handbook of meeting science* (pp. 177–202). New York, NY: Cambridge University Press.
3. https://www.bbc.com/news/magazine-17512040

Chapter 1

1. Byham, T. M., & Wellins, R. S. (2015). *Your first leadership job: How catalyst leaders bring out the best in others*. Hoboken, New Jersey: John Wiley & Sons.
2. https://www.gallup.com/services/182138/state-american-manager.aspx
3. https://hbr.org/2016/12/what-great-managers-do-daily
4. Dahling, J. J., Taylor, S. R., Chau, S. L., & Dwight, S. A. (2016). Does coaching matter? A multilevel model linking managerial coaching skill and frequency to sales goal attainment. *Personnel Psychology*, *69*(4), 863–894.
5. https://twitter.com/adammgrant/status/1396808117069963275?lang=en
6. https://knowyourteam.com/blog/2019/10/10/the-5-mistakes-youre-making-in-your-one-on-one-meetings-with-direct-reports/
7. Kahana, E., Bhatta, T., Lovegreen, L. D., Kahana, B., & Midlarsky, E. (2013). Altruism, helping, and volunteering: Pathways to well-being in late life. *Journal of Aging and Health*, *25*(1), 159–187. https://doi.org/10.1177/0898264312469665
8. Sneed, R. S., & Cohen, S. (2013). A prospective study of volunteerism and hypertension risk in older adults. *Psychology and Aging*, *28*(2), 578–586. https://doi.org/10.1037/a0032718

Chapter 2

1. DeMare, G. (1989). Communicating: The key to establishing good working relationships. *Price Waterhouse Review*, *33*, 30–37.
2. https://en.wikipedia.org/wiki/Chinese_whispers

Chapter 3

1. https://hypercontext.com/wp-content/uploads/2019/11/soapbox-state-of-one-on-ones-report.pdf

Chapter 4

1. Csikszentmihalyi, M. (1975). *Beyond boredom and anxiety*. San Francisco: Jossey-Bass.
2. Csikszentmihalyi, M. (1997). Flow and education. *NAMTA Journal, 22*(2), 2–35.
3. Ceja, L., & Navarro, J. (2011). Dynamic patterns of flow in the workplace: Characterizing within-individual variability using a complexity science approach. *Journal of Organizational Behavior, 32*(4), 627–651.
4. Emerson, H. (1998). Flow and occupation: A review of the literature. *Canadian Journal of Occupational Therapy, 65*(1), 37–44.
5. Jett, Q. R., & George, J. M. (2003). Work interrupted: A closer look at the role of interruptions in organizational life. *The Academy of Management Review, 28*(3), 494–507.

Chapter 5

1. Künn, S., Palacios, J., & Pestel, N. (2019). Indoor air quality and cognitive performance.
2. Park, R. J., Goodman, J., Hurwitz, M., & Smith, J. (2020). Heat and learning. *American Economic Journal: Economic Policy, 12*(2), 306–339.
3. Jahncke, H., Hygge, S., Halin, N., Green, A. M., & Dimberg, K. (2011). Open-plan office noise: Cognitive performance and restoration. *Journal of Environmental Psychology, 31*(4), 373–382.
4. Okken, V., Van Rompay, T., & Pruyn, A. (2013). Room to move: On spatial constraints and self-disclosure during intimate conversations. *Environment and behavior, 45*(6), 737–760.
5. Meyers-Levy, J., & Zhu, R. (2007). The influence of ceiling height: The effect of priming on the type of processing that people use. *Journal of Consumer Research, 34*(2), 174–186
6. Cohen, M. A., Rogelberg, S. G., Allen, J. A., & Luong, A. (2011). Meeting design characteristics and attendee perceptions of staff/team meeting quality. *Group Dynamics: Theory, Research, and Practice, 15*(1), 90–104. https://doi.org/10.1037/a0021549
7. Shi, T. (2013). The use of color in marketing: Colors and their physiological and psychological implications. *Berkeley Scientific Journal, 17*(1), 16.

8. Clayton, R., Thomas, C., & Smothers, J. (2015, August 5). How to do walking meetings right. *Harvard Business Review*. Retrieved from https://hbr.org/2015/08/how-to-do-walking-meetings-right
9. https://www.sciencedaily.com/releases/2014/06/140612114627.htm

Chapter 6

1. https://sloanreview.mit.edu/article/leading-remotely-requires-new-communication-strategies/

Chapter 7

1. Blanchard, K., & Ridge, G. (2009). *Helping people win at work: A business philosophy called "Don't mark my paper, help me get an A"*. FT Press.

Chapter 8

1. Byham, T. M., & Wellins, R. S. (2015). *Your first leadership job: How catalyst leaders bring out the best in others*. John Wiley & Sons.
2. Judge, T. A., Piccolo, R. F., & Ilies, R. (2004). The forgotten ones? The validity of consideration and initiating structure in leadership research. *Journal of Applied Psychology*, *89*(1), 36–51.
3. https://www.forbes.com/sites/joefolkman/2013/12/19/the-best-gift-leaders-can-give-honest-feedback/?sh=551c3b194c2b

Chapter 9

1. Newman, A., Donohue, R., & Eva, N. (2017). Psychological safety: A systematic review of the literature. *Human Resource Management Review*, *27*(3), 521–535.
2. Castro, D. R., Anseel, F., Kluger, A. N., Lloyd, K. J., & Turjeman-Levi, Y. (2018). Mere listening effect on creativity and the mediating role of psychological safety. *Psychology of Aesthetics, Creativity, and the Arts*, *12*(4), 489.
3. Zenger, J., & Folkman, J. (2014, January 15). Your employees want the negative feedback you hate to give. *Harvard Business Review*.
4. Fisher, C. D. (1979). Transmission of positive and negative feedback to subordinates: A laboratory investigation. *Journal of Applied Psychology*, *64*(5), 533–540.

5. Zenger, J., & Folkman, J. (2014, January 15). Your employees want the negative feedback you hate to give. *Harvard Business Review*.
6. Bond, C. F., Jr., & Anderson, E. L. (1987). The reluctance to transmit bad news: Private discomfort or public display?. *Journal of Experimental Social Psychology*, *23*(2), 176–187.
7. Minnikin, A., Beck, J. W., & Shen, W. (2021). Why do you ask? The effects of perceived motives on the effort that managers allocate toward delivering feedback. *Journal of Business and Psychology*, 1–18.
8. Zenger, J., & Folkman, J. (2014, January 15). Your employees want the negative feedback you hate to give. *Harvard Business Review*.
9. https://marshallgoldsmith.com/articles/teaching-leaders-what-to-stop/
10. https://www.glassdoor.com/employers/blog/employers-to-retain-half-of-their-employees-longer-if-bosses-showed-more-appreciation-glassdoor-survey/
11. https://www.pnas.org/doi/10.1073/pnas.0913149107
12. https://journals.sagepub.com/doi/abs/10.1177/2167702615611073
13. https://www.ncbi.nlm.nih.gov/pmc/articles/PMC7375895/
14. https://journals.sagepub.com/doi/10.1177/0898264310388272
15. https://www.tandfonline.com/doi/full/10.1080/00224545.2015.1095706

Chapter 10

1. Rosenthal, R., & Babad, E. Y. (1985). Pygmalion in the gymnasium. *Educational Leadership*, *43*(1), 36–39.
2. Kahneman, D., Fredrickson, B. L., Schreiber, C. A., & Redelmeier, D. A. (1993). When more pain is preferred to less: Adding a better end. *Psychological Science*, *4*(6), 401–405.

Chapter 11

1. Baldoni, J. (2010). *Lead your boss: The subtle art of managing up*. Amacom Books.
2. Nadler, A. (1997). Personality and help seeking. In *Sourcebook of social support and personality* (pp. 379–407). Springer, Boston, MA.
3. Geller, D., & Bamberger, P. A. (2012). The impact of help seeking on individual task performance: The moderating effect of help seekers' logics of action. *Journal of Applied Psychology*, *97*(2), 487.
4. https://marshallgoldsmith.com/articles/try-feedforward-instead-feedback/

Chapter 12

1. Amabile, T., & Kramer, S. (2011). *The progress principle: Using small wins to ignite joy, engagement, and creativity at work*. Harvard Business Press.

2. https://marshallgoldsmith.com/articles/questions-that-make-a-difference-the-daily-question-process/
3. https://dialoguereview.com/six-daily-questions-winning-leaders/

Chapter 13

1. Myers, D. G. (1980). *The inflated self.* New York: Seabury Press.

Chapter 15

1. Parkinson, C. N., & Osborn, R. C. (1957). *Parkinson's law, and other studies in administration* (Vol. 24). Boston: Houghton Mifflin. Also see http://www.economist.com/node/14116121
2. Karau, S. J., & Kelly, J. R. (1992). The effects of time scarcity and time abundance on group performance quality and interaction process. *Journal of Experimental Social Psychology, 28*(6), 542–571.
3. Simms, A., & Nichols, T. (2014). Social loafing: A review of the literature. *Journal of Management, 15*(1), 58–67.
4. Aubé, C., Rousseau, V., & Tremblay, S. (2011). Team size and quality of group experience: The more the merrier? *Group Dynamics: Theory, Research, and Practice, 15*(4), 357.
5. Bailenson, J. N. (2021). Nonverbal overload: a theoretical argument for the causes of zoom fatigue. *Technology, Mind, and Behavior, 2*(1).
6. Barsade, S. G., Coutifaris, C. G., & Pillemer, J. (2018). Emotional contagion in organizational life. *Research in Organizational Behavior, 38*, 137–151.
7. Grawitch, M. J., Munz, D. C., Elliott, E. K., & Mathis, A. (2003). Promoting creativity in temporary problem-solving groups: The effects of positive mood and autonomy in problem definition on idea-generating performance. *Group Dynamics: Theory, Research, and Practice, 7*(3), 200–213.
8. Heslin, P. A. (2009). Better than brainstorming? Potential contextual boundary conditions to brainwriting for idea generation in organizations. *Journal of Occupational and Organizational Psychology, 82*(1), 129–145.

Index

For the benefit of digital users, indexed terms that span two pages (e.g., 52–53) may, on occasion, appear on only one of those pages.

Boxes are indicated by *b* following the page number